The Cat Drank Milk.
The Cat With The Black Tail Drank Cold Milk.
200+ Sentence Templates For Developing ESL Writers

Jeremy Penna & MaryEllen Cathcart

Branton Press

Branton Press is an independent publishing house located in northern
Delaware focusing on basic, vintage, and critical editions of works of
fiction, poetry, and drama as well as academic and educational materials. We also publish original work by new and established authors.

Inquiries: Brantonpublishing@gmail.com

The Cat Drank Milk. The Cat With The Black Tail Drank Cold Milk.
Printed in the United States of America
Newark, Delaware
Copyright © 2023 Jeremy Penna, Mary Ellen Cathcart
All rights reserved.
ISBN-13: 978-1-950299-10-2

Library of Congress Control Number:

For Our Students

Table of Contents

Introduction (for Teachers)	1
Introduction (for Students)	5
Summary of Verb Tenses	14
Simple Present Tense	16
Present Progressive Tense	32
Simple Past Tense	48
Past Progressive Tense	64
Present Perfect Tense	80
Present Perfect Progressive Tense	96
Past Perfect Tense	112
Past Perfect Progressive Tense	128
Simple Future Tense	144
Future Progressive Tense	158
Future Perfect Tense	172
Adjective Clauses	186
Basic Time Clauses	188
Types of Frequency	190
Facts and Stative Verbs	194
Probability and Certainty (Positive)	196
Probability and Certainty (Negative)	198
The Three Cans	200
Coulda, Shoulda, Woulda, Will	202
Talking About Duration....	206
Present, Past, and Future...	208
Gerunds vs Infinitives: The Basics	212
Using Gerunds After Prepositions	213
A Few Tricky Words	217
Special Expressions	219
Passive Voice	221
When do we Use the Passive?	223
Prepositions of Place	226
Prepositions of Time	228
Inseparable Phrasal Verbs	230
Separable Phrasal Verbs	232
Phrasals with Common Verbs	234
Most Common Irregular Verbs	238
Most Common Irregular Verbs	239

INTRODUCTION (FOR TEACHERS)

This is a book.
This is an ESL book.
This is an ESL book designed to help students.
This is an ESL book designed to help students write better sentences.

This is an ESL book designed to help students write better sentences through repetition.

The assumption here is a simple one. ESL students need to practice writing. One way to practice writing is to work on sentences. Improving writing by drilling sentences parallels the idea of practice in many other disciplines. Musicians don't start with songs. They drill notes and chords. Basketball players don't start with games. They drill dribbling and shooting. ESL writers—all writers—would benefit by drilling sentences.

Students sometimes skip that step. One general definition of what "practicing writing" means is expressing ideas. Write a paragraph about your hometown. Summarize an article in a newspaper. Write a comparison-contrast essay explaining two different points of view about a film. Sit beside a lake and write three paragraphs of description in which you engage all five senses. All teachers are familiar with the stock assignments. They are useful. They hone critical thinking skills, reward clarity, and demand the sorts of cohesion—harmony of part and part, and part and whole—which are key to effective discourse. Being able to explain, to describe, to compare, to persuade are essential competencies, and the stock assignments go a long way to helping students master them.

Unfortunately, ESL students often have more basic needs. Many of them struggle simply to put words together in the right order, to make subjects and objects agree, or find the right tense. The stock assignments sometimes ask them to do too much too soon. Often, they approach them in a way that teachers ought to sympathize with. Given the task of, for example, of summarizing an article about the dangers of obesity, they first "think of their ideas"—usually in their native language: unfortunate for health is the obesity people. They say, "now how would I say this in English?" They translate, proof-read, and turn in the assignment.

The instructor returns the assignment with mistakes underlined in red, along with suggestions along the lines of: "you need to learn the conditional." An ideal student goes back, fixes the mistakes, and tries to understand why they're mistakes. A less ideal student looks at the red underlines, grumbles, shrugs, and makes the same mistakes again. All of us who have taught—all of us, myself included, who have been that student—are familiar with this process.

The problem, of course, is that "expressing ideas" is not the same as "mastering structures." ESL students have good ideas—or ideas that are as good as those of their domestic counterparts. They do not have—and in many cases will not have for a number of years—a natural ear for sentences, a feel for the comfortable rhythms of prose, or familiarity with the ordinary structures of the language. It bears repeating that structures are different from ideas, since grammar is different from semantics. Semantically, colorless green ideas do not and cannot sleep furiously. Grammatically, however, they do and can. This is an old cliché.

The generic Rx for structural problems is the grammar exercise—often some variation on "fill-in-the-blank." The student is given a sentence like, "The man_____ (walk)" and has to supply walks or walked or has walked depending on the point being trained. These exercises are useful in getting students to understand and apply the rules and probably will always be a big.

Introduction (for Teachers)

big part of ESL grammar lessons. At the same time, it's almost universally recognized that these exercises aren't enough. They're monotonous and train a task which students almost never have to do in real life. When, outside of a grammar book or a signature line, will they be asked to fill in a blank? The rules of grammar are, after all, meant to be generative rather than restrictive. They enable speakers to produce their own sentences, to multiply and bear fruit as they pursue a line of thought through the theoretically limitless channels supplied by the form. The point of a generative model like this is to train students in grammar. Too often students, wrestling with the meaning of the words, revert to the more comfortable grammatical structures of their native languages. This book attempts, in some ways, to divorce the two competencies and train the former.

The idea of using templates in order to encourage students to practice these forms is hardly original. I first encountered the exercise in Jerry Morris's Seven Sentence Building Activities to Develop Advanced Writers (Collins, 2010). I used the Morris's book for several semesters and found the activities pleasant and easy to incorporate. A more well-known example, particularly among composition teachers is Berkenstein and Graff's They Say, I Say (Norton, 2005), which uses generic templates to teach the rhetorical moves common in academic writing. Where The Cat Drank Milk seeks to differentiate itself is in targeting, in a more comprehensive way, the specific needs of the low-to-mid level ESL writer (A2-B1 in CEFR terms). Morris's templates are creative and interesting, but the book is really designed for developing a sense of style among populations of native speakers who struggle with the ability to coordinate longer sentences. They Say, I Say, extraordinarily helpful for upper-level ESL students tiptoeing into academic writing for the first time but is too advanced for a target population which, in many cases, has not yet mastered the more elementary grammatical structures in English.

Given that population, the organization of The Cat Drank Milk has been designed to allow for multiple approaches. The first half of the book is organized by verb tense. The chapters begin with a basic explanation of the rules for each tense, followed by several warm-up activities, and examples of conjugations in the declarative, negative, and interrogative. Following this are a series of staggered sentence templates helping students to write their own sentences by providing models. These sentences begin at the most basic level—subject, verb, object: the cat drank milk—and then add layers of complexity by gradually adding additional elements. The cat drank milk. The cat with the black tail drank cold milk. The cat with the black tail drank cold milk from a porcelain bowl. This exercise is then repeated using negative, interrogative, conditional, and modal forms of the same sentence. Through all of this, students are given ample space to produce a variety of practice sentences. Finally, the chapter concludes with a brief "practical application" section, comprising a short reading passage and a writing challenge. The reading passage is designed to demonstrate to students the real-world situations in which the modeled grammar structures might ordinarily be used, and the writing challenge is meant to allow students a chance to practice more extended writing in response to the model.

The second half of the book contains a series of supplementary explanations and exercises: traditional fill-in-the-blank and complete-the-sentence activities intended to provide the students more complete sense of the structural elements which are drilled in the sentence-practice section. Though we admit that these exercises are often somewhat banal, it did seem necessary to fill in some of the gaps from the first section: irregular verb forms, gerunds & infinitives, adjective clauses, prepositions, etc. We intend this to be more or less a reference section.

The number of templates and the volume of supplementary material allows this book to be used in a variety of ways. The simplest is perhaps to go through the book in order: tense by tense, template by template, starting with the simplest sentences and advancing through the more difficult ones. This progression, however, can be adjusted to suit the needs and goals of both teacher and student. Lower-level students might find it better to only do the Level One and Level Two sentences. Students who are just beginning to learn to differentiate verb tenses and sentence patterns tend to need a good deal of repetition before they're ready for additional layers of complexity. Higher level students, on the other hand, may wish to skip the first two levels and practice only with Levels Three and Four. In my own classroom practice, I have found the templates to be a useful warm-up activity in preparation for more intensive content. For example, during a lesson in which "frequency" is a key idea, I might have the students write ten sentences using the simple present templates. Noun always verbs. Noun sometimes verbs. Noun rarely verbs, verbs, or verbs. This primes their brains and gets them ready to use the main grammatical structure of the day, a structure which can then be explored more fully over the course of the class.

There are both benefits and limitations to this approach. One straightforward and immediate benefit is that students are forced to scrutinize sentence patterns and parts of speech. To follow the templates, they have to quickly parse what the noun is, what the verb is, and what the object is. This forces them to pay attention to the grammatical relationship between parts. Perhaps surprisingly, students don't seem to mind this. In fact, I have found that my own students tend to enjoy sentence practice. It's not onerous. It provides a low-pressure opportunity to improve some basic skills. And, best of all, imagination is often given a chance for free play. It's not uncommon, in my own classroom, to see students break into giggles at the sentences that they come up with. The instructor, of course, can (and probably should) keep the giggles going—even at the risk of traipsing into silliness or Mad-libs style non-sequiturs. Funny things are often memorable, and we want students, after all, to remember. A nonsensical sentence that follows the rules can internalize habits of construction just as well as a sensible one can. One of my own students recently came up with: "While the long-haired teacher was jumping on the trampoline and drinking tequila, the diligent students were drinking tequila and doing their grammar homework." Everyone laughed. No tequila was drunk.

The limitations of the book are two-fold. Most obviously, there are very few "task-based" activities. Students are not directed to use English to solve problems and negotiate situations in the real world or prompted to perform the sorts of academic assignments (locate a main idea, organize a paragraph) common in intensive English programs. This book trains only a specific task (writing sentences) and is therefore probably best used as part of a curriculum which challenges the students to use language in a wider variety of ways according to their academic or personal goals. A second limitation has to do with the redundant nature of the sentence practice itself. Students will often produce sentences quite close to the template sentences and with errors which the structure of the templates do not prevent. For example, for the template sentence "the cat drank milk," students, often enough, will produce sentences like: "the dog drank waters." While the argument could be made that producing even these sorts of sentences is beneficial since certain target competencies (word order, verb tense) are improved, the potential for such missteps probably necessitates a good deal of instructor intervention. The teacher will have to actively participate in the sentence building process both to catch errors and to encourage the students to imaginatively explore ways to stretch the templates. One fairly easy way that I've accomplished the latter task is by providing students a "daily theme" for sentence practice: e.g., all sentences, for a particular day, should be about cooking or about sports or about occupations. This is often a stimulating challenge and prevents the practice sentences from becoming too derivative.

A final eccentricity of this book—I'm not sure whether or not to call it a limitation—deserves mentioning. Both students and teachers will notice that almost all the sample templates involve animals. Cats drink milk. Dogs bark and wag their tails. Dolphins swim, etc, etc, etc. When reviewing early drafts, several of my colleagues remarked: "Don't you think it would be good to use different kinds of sentences: maybe with people or things?" Maybe, maybe not. One motivation for strictly using animals was to provide nouns and verbs of the most generic type possible, once again to encourage students to focus on structure rather than meaning. However a second motivation—maybe a sillier one—has to do with a striking and occasionally interesting gap that I have noticed in the vocabulary of many ESL students. One day, while teaching a class in Political Science for rather upper-level university students I casually asked my students if they knew what noises cats made in English. My students—all of whom could read at roughly a university level—were surprised and amused to learn that when they're hungry, they meow; when they're happy, they purr; when they're annoyed, they hiss; and, when they're "in love" they yowl. The last item in the list led to a spirited discussion among several of my students from rural areas in South America about what a truly sleep-shattering noise this can be, one which, thankfully, they only rarely heard in the United States. "Is it because American cats don't fall in love?" Gales of laughter. In any event, my students, who could often write with great subtlety on academic topics did not know that snakes slither, that puppies yip, that horses gallop, and that giraffes crane their necks. "My," I thought, "there ought to be a book." The last semester that I used this book, I was very pleased that a number of my students had begun referring to it as "that cat book" or "that animal book." In an ESL marketplace which includes with seemingly countless textbooks identical in style and method, it gives us a modest pleasure to have authored one of a handful which might conceivably double as a bestiary.

Introduction (for Teachers)

In conclusion, we hope you and your students thoroughly enjoy "The Cat Drank Milk." This book stands out with a unique linguistic lens, addressing the nuanced relationship between semantics and syntax, and emphasizing that grammar is generative, not restrictive. By focusing on sentence templates, we aim to help ESL learners master the art of construction while unleashing their creative potential within the realm of grammar. We believe this distinctive approach will prove immensely beneficial for students, providing them with not just a set of rules but a toolkit to actively generate expressive and meaningful sentences. As teachers and learners embark on this journey together, we hope "The Cat Drank Milk" becomes a steadfast companion, fostering both skill development and a touch of whimsy in the pursuit of English language mastery.

INTRODUCTION (FOR STUDENTS)

"Grammar is like cooking. It might seem complicated, but once you understand the basic rules, you can create endless possibilities." - Jürgen Klopp"

Think of grammar like cooking, you have some basic ingredients and you combine them in different ways to get different meals. You can combine chicken and rice to make a rice dish or you can combine it to make a soup. You can change the vegetables and get countless different meals from the same basic ingredients. Similarily, in grammar, modifying the components like sentence structure, word choice, or punctuation can yield a wide range of expressions and written compositions.

In this introduction, we'll delve into the building blocks of language, starting with the essence of words and phrases. Once we've crafted sentences, we won't stop there – we'll venture further into the intricacies of clauses, exploring how each element contributes to the richness of expression. So, buckle up as we navigate through words, phrases, clauses, and sentences, unlocking the true potential of grammar step by step."

What do you think the most basic ingredient or unit in grammar?

1._____

If you guessed the word, you are correct! The most basic unit of grammar is the word. A word is a fundamental unit of language that carries meaning. It is a combination of sounds or letters that represents a concept, object, action, or idea. Words can belong to different parts of speech. These words can be grouped to form phrases. Sometimes, a phrase may only contain a single word. Finally, we can combine these phrases to make complete sentences. Let's go over each of these components to see how they stack up.

Basic Building Blocks: Words

Every word is a part of speech. The parts of speech are categories into which words are classified based on their grammatical functions and roles within sentences. Can you thik of some categoies?

1._____
2._____
3._____
4._____
5._____

There are six major parts of speech:

1. **Noun:** A noun is a word that represents a person, place, thing, or idea. For example: "dog."
2. **Verb:** A verb is a word that describes an action, occurrence, or state of being. For example: "run."
3. **Adjective:** An adjective is a word that modifies or describes a noun. For example "happy."
4. **Adverb**: An adverb is a word that modifies or describes a verb, adjective, or another adverb. For example "quickly."
5. **Preposition:** A preposition is a word that shows a relationship between a noun (or pronoun) and other words in a sentence. For example "in."
6. **Conjunction:** A conjunction is a word that connects words, phrases, or clauses within a sentence. For example "and."

Introduction (for Students)

In the world of language, words are like puzzle pieces, and parts of speech are the tools that help us fit them together. Nouns, verbs, adjectives, adverbs, prepositions, and conjunctions are the special building blocks that allow us to create sentences and express ourselves. Parts of speech act as the rules guiding how words can fit, ensuring that our expressions make sense. For example, you wouldn't say 'elephant quickly,' because the parts of speech don't connect. These parts of speech provide a framework for understanding the roles and functions of words in sentences, enabling us to construct meaningful and grammatically correct expressions.

How is a Sentence Made?

Now that we've explored the fundamental pieces of language words, let's shift our focus to how these pieces come together to create meaningful expressions. A sentence, serves as a unit of language that conveys a complete thought or idea. Which of the following are sentences or complete thoughts?

1. The kitten naps.
2. Walking in the park.
3. A blue parrot.
4. Sat by the window.

If you guessed that only the first one was a complete sentence, you are correct. In 'The kitten naps,' we have a complete thought—it tells us something specific about the kitten and what it's doing. However, in 'Walking in the park,' we encounter a phrase, not a complete thought on its own. It lacks a subject leaving us wondering who is walking.. Similarly, 'A blue parrot' and 'Sat by the window' are also not complete thoughts. Although they provide information, they are missing crucial information. They leave us curious about the parrot's action or more details about the scene.

Sentences are composed of several key elements that work together to form a grammatically correct and meaningful statement. Based upon the last exercise, what do you think a sentence should minimally have? It's ok if you don't what it's called, do your best to describe what it is.

Hint: There are only two main components.

1._____
2._____

Sentneces have two main elements, the subject and the predicate. In English, the subject is a noun phrase that performs the action or is the main focus of the sentence. It is the topic of the sentence or what the sentence is about. The predicate is the verb phrase that describes the action or state of the subject. It provides information about what the subject is doing or the characteristics attributed to the subject. Sentences can also include other elements such as adverbs, prepositional phrases, conjunctions, and more, to provide further details, clarify relationships, or connect ideas.

In grammar, we find subjects and predicates inside something called a 'phrase.' A phrase is like a team of words working together in a sentence. It's a word, or a group of words that that functions as a unit within a sentence. To make a simple sentence, we need a subject or a noun phrase, like 'The tiger,' and a predicate or a verb phrase, like 'pounced.' Put them together, and we get the sentence 'The tiger pounced.' This way of organizing words helps us express ideas clearly.

Can you make a simple sentence? Ensure each sentence has a subject, predicate, and expresses a complete thought.

1._____.

Introduction (for Students)

Now, as we dig deeper into constructing sentences, let's uncover a handy tool called generative rules. These rules are like blueprints that guide us in building sentences. One way to use these rules is by understanding the structure of a sentence. For instance, look at our earlier sentence 'The tiger pounced.' We can represent this structure more formally by following a simple pattern, like a set of instructions. In this case, we say 'S → NP VP,' which means a Sentence (S) is made up of a Noun Phrase (NP) and a Verb Phrase (VP). Let's explore how these rules become our language-building blocks, allowing us to create a variety of sentences with ease.

S → NP VP
NP → The tiger
VP → pounced

The tiger pounced.

By using generative rules and combining verb phrases and noun phrases we are able to express complete thoughts. Nevertheless, we still need to figure out how to make words into phrases that we can put into sentences.

The Noun Phrase

Now that we've explored the basics of sentences, let's zoom in on the first essential component: the noun phrase. Noun phrases play a crucial role as they are the subjects in sentences. However, they can also be found in other phrases like verb phrases or preposition phrases. In its simplest form, a noun phrase must contain either a noun or a pronoun. And remember, a pronoun is a word that takes the place of a noun, like 'he' or 'she.'

As we continue our exploration of noun phrases, let's reinforce our understanding with a closer look at generative rules. These rules, which we've previously touched upon, act as our guides, helping us structure sentences effectively. For example, consider the noun 'Hyenas' or the pronoun 'They.' We've learned that we can represent these structures using a simple rule: NP → N, where NP stands for Noun Phrase and N represents the noun. This tool, already part of our language construction kit, enables us to build a variety of noun phrases.

NP → N

Now that we've got our language construction tools, let's add more elements to our phrases.. We can make noun phrases more interesting by including articles or possessives. Here's a handy rule: NP can be made up of an article (like 'the' or 'a') and a noun. The rule looks like this: NP → (Art) N. The parentheses means that the element is optional. Using this, we can create sentences like 'The hyena,' 'My cat,' or just 'Cats.'

NP → (Art) N

This rule can generate the following sentences:

The hyena
My cat
Cats

1. _____ _____
    Art   *Noun*

2. _____ _____
    Art   *Noun*

3. _____ _____
    Art   *Noun*

Now that we're sentence builders, let's add more details to our subjects. Noun phrases can become even more specific with prepositional phrases. Recall that prepositions tell us the relationship between two nouns. Therefore, a prepositional phrase has a preposition and another noun phrase. So, using the rule NP → N (PP), where NP is Noun Phrase, N is the noun, and (PP) means a prepositional phrase, we can make subjects more detailed.

7

Introduction (for Students)

PP → P NP

NP → N (PP)

The hyena in the jungle

1. _____ _____
   Noun   PP
2. _____ _____
   Noun   PP
3. _____ _____
   Noun   PP

As we keep building our sentences, let's make our subjects more descriptive. Noun phrases can contain describing words called adjectives. It's like adding colors to our sentences. And here's something fun – we can have not just one, but a bunch of adjectives together. We show this with a star symbol (*). So, the rule is NP → (Adj*) N, where NP is Noun Phrase, Adj is the adjective, and the star means we can have one or more adjectives.

NP → (Adj*) N

Ugly, hungry hyenas

1. _____ _____
   Adj   Noun
2. _____ _____
   Adj   Noun
3. _____ _____ _____
   Adj   Adj   Noun

We can combine each of these rules to make a master rule. NP → (Art) (Adj*) N (PP). Let's break it down. NP means Noun Phrase, the core of our sentence. (Art) is like adding 'the' or 'a' for specifics. (Adj*) lets you include describing words, making it more specific. N is just the noun – the main character. (PP) adds extra details with prepositional phrases. It's like a recipe for noun phrases where you can mix and match to craft your own unique expressions.

NP → (Art) (Adj*) N (PP)

The angry hyenas in the jungle

1. _____ _____ _____
   Art   Adj   Noun
2. _____ _____ _____
   Adj   Noun   PP
3. _____ _____ _____ _____
   Art   Adj   Noun   PP

As we wrap up our exploration of noun phrases, remember, these aren't just rules; they're the keys to unlock your sentence creativity. The ability to craft sentences isn't about memorizing, but understanding the tools in our language construction kit. Whether it's adding details with articles, adjectives, or prepositions, you're the architect of your sentences. Now that you can confidently build sentence subjects, let's shift our focus to the action of the sentence, the verb phrase.

The Verb Phrase

Now, let's dive into the dynamic world of verb phrases. These are the powerhouse of sentences, bringing action and life to our words. At their core, verb phrases must include, at the very least, a verb. Let's kick things off with a simple example: 'Run!'"

To break it down further, we use a simple formula to represent verb phrases:

VP → V.

VP, representing Verb Phrase, can be written as V, where V is the essential verb. So, in essence, VP → V serves as our guiding principle for constructing verb phrases.

Can you think of some more examples of verbs that can be a whole verb phrase?

But there's more we can add to verb phrases. We can sprinkle in extra details to modify the action, giving our sentences depth and nuance. Check out this formula: VP → (Adv) V (PP) (Adv), where Adv stands for adverbs and PP for prepositional phrases. These optional elements enhance the verb, allowing us to express actions with precision. For instance:

VP → (Adv) V (PP) (Adv)

Crouch quietly!
Hide under the bed!
Run across the road quickly!

1. _____V_____ _____Adv_____

2. _____V_____ _____PP_____

3. _____V_____ _____PP_____ _____Adv_____

Verbs can work with noun phrases in different ways, shown by the formula VP → V (NP) (NP). It depends on the specific verb if it needs a noun phrase as an object. Some verbs, like 'Dance!', stand alone, while others, like 'Eat your dinner!', need an object. Interestingly, certain verbs, like 'Give the dog a bone,' can even have two objects.

VP → V (NP) (NP)

Dance!
Eat your dinner!
Give the dog a bone.

1. _____V_____

2. _____V_____ _____NP_____

3. _____V_____ _____NP_____ _____NP_____

Some verb phrases can include infinitival verb phrases, which start with 'to.' This allows for additional layers of meaning in our sentences. Check out the formula: VP → to VP or VP → V (VP). Here are examples:

VP → to VP
VP → V (VP)

Want to pounce on the mouse.
Want to learn to pounce on the mouse

1. _____V_____ to _____VP_____

2. _____V_____ to _____VP_____

3. _____V_____ to _____VP_____

To create verb phrases, we can combine these rules into the versatile formula for verb phrases (VP): VP → (Adv) V (NP) (NP) (PP) (Adv). This formula, like a set of building blocks, empowers us to construct verb phrases in countless ways, adding depth and nuance to our expressions.

VP → (Adv) V (NP) (NP) (PP) (Adv)

Now that you can describe the who and the what of sentences in countless ways, you're well on your way to constructing an infinite array of sentences in English. Your sentence-building skills are expanding, and the possibilities are endless.

Putting it all Together

Now that we've got the awesome tools for both noun phrases and verb phrases, let's join forces and create some magic – sentences! We've got our master formulas ready:

For verb phrases, it's like a secret recipe:

VP → (Adv) V (NP) (NP) (PP) (Adv) or VP → (Adv) V (VP) (PP) (Adv).

- Noun phrases bring in their own charm with

NP → (Art) (Adj*) N (PP).

And when we combine our noun phrases and verb phrases, voila! We get a full sentence:

S → NP VP

Similar to a math forumla, we can rewrite these rules to their end words. We can pick and choose the noun phrases and verb phrases that we want to use to make a simple sentence. For example, from the above rules, we can choose these noun phrases and verb phrases respectively, and then rewrite the sentence rule as follows.

NP → Art Adj N
VP → Adv V VP PP
S → Art Adj N Adv V PP

The hungry hyena quietly crounched behind the tree.

Breaking down sentences into their basic components, we use formulas like S → Art Adj N Adv V PP. Each element, such as Art (article), Adj (adjective), N (noun), Adv (adverb), V (verb), and PP (prepositional phrase), represents a distinct part of speech that we can customize in our sentences. It's like plugging values into a math equation – choosing specific words for each element creates a complete sentence. By applying these rules, we rewrite the sentence formula with specific words, allowing us to generate a variety of sentences, similar to rewriting a math formula to create different equations.

This process empowers us to construct an array of sentences, each with its unique flavor and meaning, by selecting different elements for our NP and VP variables. It's the linguistic equivalent of rewriting a math formula to generate various equations, offering endless possibilities for expressing our thoughts in English. Deconstructing sentences into the noun phrase and the verb phrase reveals formulas that act as blueprints for crafting creative and diverse sentences. These generative formulas showcase the versatility of a few fundamental parts of speech.

Grammar rules, rather than being rigid constraints, serve as valuable tools that empower us to construct sentences with ease. They provide structure and coherence, acting as scaffolding that supports and enhances the art of communication. Grammar facilitates language skills, enabling clear and accurate expression. It's important to note that the variations introduced here are just a starting point, not an exhaustive list. More complex structures like adjective clauses or noun clauses will be explored in later sections as your understanding of the English language progresses.

Introduction (for Students)

THE NOUN PHRASE

THE VERB PHRASE

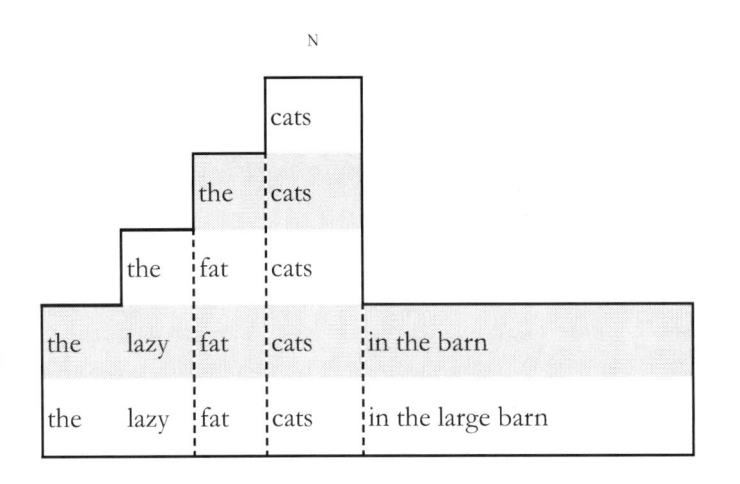

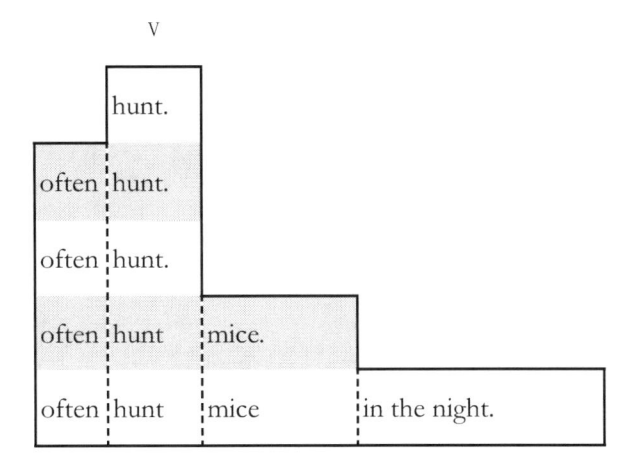

		N		
		cats		
	the	cats		
	the	fat	cats	
the	lazy	fat	cats	in the barn
the	lazy	fat	cats	in the large barn

	V		
	hunt.		
often	hunt.		
often	hunt.		
often	hunt	mice.	
often	hunt	mice	in the night.

Can you make 10 sentences from this?

1. _____
2. _____
3. _____
4. _____
5. _____
6. _____
7. _____
8. _____
9. _____
10. _____

Introduction (for Students)

Building Bigger Sentences

If you're thinking that there's more to sentences than just the simple ones we've discussed, you're absolutely correct. Beyond simple sentences, we have a fundamental concept called "clauses," which serve as another essential building block in the construction of more intricate sentences.

To understand this, picture it like a series of nesting Russian dolls. In this analogy, words are the smallest units, coming together to form phrases. These phrases, in turn, combine to create clauses, and finally, clauses join forces to craft complete sentences. Each building block serves as a critical component, working in harmony to construct a sentence that is not only structurally sound but also rich in meaning.

It's crucial to grasp the flexibility inherent in constructing sentences. Every linguistic component, be it a phrase, a clause, or even an entire sentence, can exhibit remarkable versatility. A phrase is not confined to multiple words; it can be as concise as a single word. Similarly, a clause can stand alone with just one phrase, and a sentence can consist of a solitary clause. This interconnected hierarchy allows for a dynamic and versatile language structure, ensuring that simplicity or complexity is a matter of choice, not limitation.

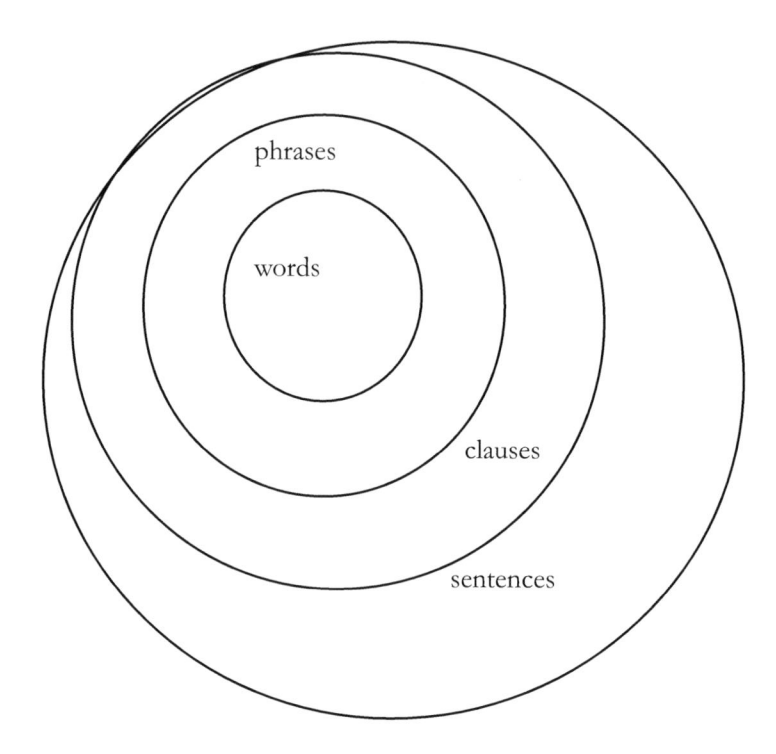

In order to make longer and more complex sentences, we combine simple sentences or clauses. Recall that when discussing parts of speech, we mentioned conjunctions. Conjuctions help us connect multiple clausses to create a bigger sentence. Take the conjunction "and". We can join any two simple sentences together to create a new sentence as follows.

The bird sings.
The cat sleeps.
The bird sings and the cat sleeps.

Introduction (for Students)

We can write this as a sentence is made of a clause followed by a conjunction plus another clause.

S → Cl Conj Cl

Can you put two simple sentences together with the conjunction "and"?

1. _____
      Clause

2. _____
      Clause

3. _____ and _____.
      Clause   *Clause*

This is often referred to as a compound sentence and the class of conjunctions used in this structure can be abbreviated as FANBOYS (for and nor but or yet so). These typically join two clauses on equal footing. This allows us to connect two simple sentences and make an infinite amount of new sentences.

Another way to join two simple sentences is to make complex sentences. In this structure, two simple sentences can be united by a conjunction, where one clause assumes the role of the main clause, and the other becomes a subordinate clause. Now, 'subordinate' might sound a bit daunting, but think of it as a supporting clause that adds conditions or context to the main clause. For instance, consider 'The bird sings if the cat is not around.' Here, the clause 'the cat is not around' acts as a condition influencing the main clause 'The bird sings.' There are various conjunctions like 'before,' 'after,' 'while,' 'as long as,' 'as soon as,' and 'when' that introduce subordinate clauses, enriching our sentences with additional layers of meaning.

The bird sings
The cat is not around.
The bird sings if the cat is not around.

Can you combine two sentences to make a complex sentence with a subordinating conjunction?

1. _____
      Clause

2. _____
      Clause

3. _____ _____ _____
      Clause   *Conj*   *Clause*

Let's recap what we've covered. We've taken a close look at the fundamental elements of sentences. We've learned about words and their function or part of speech. We've learned that words buld phrases like noun phrases (NP), which are groups of words that tell us about something or someone, and verb phrases (VP), which are made up of words that show actions or describe what's happening.

By understanding these foundational building blocks, we're able to build variety of simple sentences. Just like how different LEGO pieces can be used to create various structures, we can mix and match words, noun phrases, and verb phrases to generate countless unique sentences. In addition, we learned that we can, in turn, take these simple sentences and use them to build even bigger more complex sentences.

As you continue on your language learning journey, remember that these skills serve as your foundation. With practice, you'll not only construct sentences but also tell engaging stories and express your thoughts with clarity and confidence. Keep building your language skills, one sentence at a time!

SUMMARY OF VERB TENSES

Tense	Affirmative	Negative	Question	Use
Simple Present	Cats meow. Cats always meow.	Cats don't meow. Cats never meow.	Do cats meow?	Facts, frequency, stative verbs
Simple Past	The cat meowed yesterday.	The cat didn't meow yesterday.	Did the cat meow yesterday?	Actions completed in past.
Simple Future	The cat will meow tomorrow. The cat is going to meow tomorrow.	The cat won't meow tomorrow. The cat isn't going to meow tomorrow.	Will the cat meow tomorrow? Is the cat going to meow tomorrow?	Plans, predictions, promises, consequences, reactions
Present Progressive	The cat is meowing.	The cat isnt meowing.	Is the cat meowing?	Actions in progress right now.
Past Progressive	The cat was meowing yesterday when the dog barked.	The cat wasn't meowing yesterday when the dog barked.	Was the cat meowing yesterday when the dog barked?	Actions in progess at a specific point in the past. Interruptions. Simultaneous events.
Future Progressive	The cat will be meowing tomorrow when I come home.	The cat won't be meowing tomorrow when I come home.	Will the cat be meowing tomorrow when I come home?	Actions in progress at a specific point in the future.
Present Perfect	The cat has meowed before.	The cat hasn't meowed before.	Has the cat meowed before?	Expereriences, Duration, Repeated actions.
Past Perfect	The cat had already meowed by the time I came home.	The cat had never meowed until she saw the milk.	Had the cat ever meowed before she saw the milk?	Actions occuring before a prior action in past.
Future Perfect	The cat will have meowed by the time I get home.	The cat will not have meowed by the time I get home.	Will the cat have meowed by the time I get home?	Completed actions prior to future event.

Summary of Verb Tenses

TENSE	AFFIRMATIVE	NEGATIVE	QUESTION	USE
Present Perfect Progressive	The cat has been meowing for an hour.	The cat hasn't been meowing for very long.	How long has the cat been meowing?	Duration from the past through the present.
Past Perfect Progressive	The cat had been meowing for an hour when I came home.	The cat hadn't been mowing for every long when I came home.	How long had the cat been meowing when you came home?	Duration before specific moment in the past.
Future Perfect Progressive	The cat will have been meowing for hours when I get home.	The cat will not have been meowing for very long when I get home.	How long will the cat have been meowing when you get home?	Duration before specific moment in the future.
Real Conditional	When the cat meows, the dog barks.	When the cat doesn't meow, the dog doesn't bark.	Does the cat meow when the dog barks?	Connected actions.
Present Unreal Conditional	We don't have a cat. If we had a cat, the cat would meow.	We have a cat. If we didn't have a cat, the cat wouldn't meow.	We don't have a cat. If we had a cat, would the cat meow?	Imaginary situations.
Past Unreal Conditional	We didn't have a cat last year. If we had had a cat, the cat would have meowed.	We had a cat last year. If we hadn't had a cat, the cat wouldn't have meowed.	We didn't have a cat last year. If we had had a cat, would the cat have meowed?	Imaginary situations in the past.

Note: The future perfect progressive tense does not have a chapter in this book because it is so seldomly used.

SIMPLE PRESENT TENSE

Rules

The simple present is used for:

* Frequency
Always, usually, often, sometimes, rarely, never
I drink coffee.

drink coffee   drink coffee   drink coffee
←————|————————|————|————————|————→
drink coffee   Now   drink coffee

* Facts about the world
Birds fly. The sky is blue. Snow is cold.

*Stative verbs
Have, feel, like, love, know, agree, believe...
I love coffee.

love coffee

I.I Warm Up

What happens <u>every winter</u>?

1. Snow falls every winter.

2.

3.

What happens <u>every day</u>?

1. The sun rises every day.

2.

3.

What happens <u>every second</u>?

1. I breathe every second.

2.

3.

Simple Present Tense Forms

I	usually	work	on Monday.
He She It	sometimes	works	
You We They	often	work	

Negative Present Tense Forms

I	don't	work	on Monday.
He She It	doesn't	work	
You We They	don't	work	

Yes-No Qs Present Tense Forms

Do	I	work	on Monday?
Does	he she it	work	
Do	you we they	work	

Wh Qs Present Tense Forms

Why	do	I	work	on Monday?
What	does	he she it	work	
Where	do	you we they	work	

Simple Present Tense

Level I sentences

(One clause, adverb before verb)

Most adverbs of frequency follow the same pattern.

Level II sentences

(two clauses, joined by *when*, *whenever*, or *if*.

Level III sentences

(one clause with *only when*)

Only comes before the verb.
When comes after.

Level IV sentences

(Two clauses linked with *although*).

1. The dog <u>always</u> barks.

The _____ always _____
       noun(s)   *verb(s) + obj*

2. The dog <u>sometimes</u> barks.

The _____ sometimes _____
       noun(s)   *verb(s) + obj*

3. The dog <u>never</u> barks.

The _____ never _____
       noun(s)   *verb(s) + obj*

4. The rooster crows <u>every time</u> the sun rises.

The _____ _____ every time the _____ _____
       noun(s)   *verb(s)*   *noun(s)*   *verb(s)*

5. The rooster crows <u>whenever</u> the sun rises.

The _____ _____ whenever the _____ _____
       noun(s)   *verb(s)*   *noun(s)*   *verb(s)*

6. The cat <u>only</u> dreams <u>when</u> she sleeps.

The _____ only _____ when _____ _____
       noun(s)   *verb(s)*   *noun(s)*   *verb(s)*

7. The horse <u>only</u> gallops <u>when</u> she <u>races</u> in the summer.

The _____ only _____ when _____ _____
       noun(s)   *verb(s)*   *noun(s)*   *verb(s)*

8. <u>Although</u> the dog <u>always</u> barks, the cat <u>never</u> meows.

Although the _____ always _____
                  noun(s)   *verb(s) + obj*

the _____ never _____
       noun(s)   *verb(s) + obj*

9. <u>Although</u> the dog always <u>barks</u>, the cat <u>only</u> meows when she feels hungry.

Although the _____ always _____
                  noun(s)   *verb(s) + obj*

the _____ only _____ when _____ _____
       noun(s)   *verb(s)*   *noun(s)*   *verb(s)*

17

Simple Present Tense

LET'S ASK SOME QUESTIONS

Take a couple of your sentences from the previous page. Write four questions. Use "when" or "how often."

Examples:

When does the dog bark?
How often does the dark bark?

_____ _____ _____ _____
When/ how often   *do/ does*   *noun(s)/pronoun*   *verb?*

1. _____?
2. _____?
3. _____?
4. _____?

> Simple present often expresses frequency. Many questions start with *when* or *how often*.
>
> Examples:
>
> How often do you work out?
>
> When do you eat dinner?
>
> How often does your mother text you?
>
> When do they go to bed?

NOW ANSWER WITH A NOUN CLAUSE

Pick one of the introductory clauses below:
It doesn't matter   I don't know   It's not important   It's not clear   I can't say

Examples:

It's not clear when the dog barks.
I can't say how often the dog barks.

_____ _____ _____ _____
Introductory clause   *when/ how often*   *noun(s)*   *verbs*

Write four answers to the questions above using an introductory clause.

1. _____
2. _____
3. _____
4. _____

> Pay attention to the order of subjects and verbs!
>
> Examples:
>
> I don't know how often I work out.
>
> It doesn't matter when I eat dinner.
>
> I can't say how often my mother texts me.
>
> It's not clear when they go to bed.

Simple Present Tense

CONDITIONS AND CONSEQUENCES

Unreal Conditions
An unreal condition *imagines something different.*

→

Unreal Consequences
If we imagine that one thing is different in the past, other things change too. produce *unreal effects.*

If I worked hard......

then I would have more money.

We add conditions in two ways:
1) *I wish...*
 I never work hard.
  I wish I worked hard.
2) *If....*
  If I worked hard...
**When using *if*, we need to add a second clause introducing the unreal consequence.

We indicate unreal consequences, in the present with *would* and then the simple form of the verb.
1) I wish I worked hard.
  Then I would have more money.
2) If I worked hard,
  then I would have more money.

Warm Up

What are three things you wish?

1. I wish

2.

3.

Warm Up

What are the consequences of your wishes?

1. Then I would

2.

3.

Note: Even though the verb is in the past form, these sentences are not in the past. They are in the present tense still. Often English learners become confused because they assume the -ed ending defines the past in these cases. The unreal consequences are also in present tense.

The _____ _____ _____ I wish _____ _____
   noun/ nouns   *expression of frequency*   *verbs*   *noun(s)*   *verbed*

Then _____ _____
    noun(s)   *would verb*

Write four of your own sentences using this template. In some sentences use <u>if</u> instead of <u>I wish</u>.

1. _____

2. _____

3. _____

4 _____

Simple Present Tense

PRACTICAL APPLICATION

Read the following short paragraph. <u>Underline</u> the expressions of frequency. (Circle) the conditionals.

Who Am I?

Let me tell you a bit about myself. I consider myself somewhat of a nerd and a bookworm. I <u>always</u> have my nose in a novel. <u>Every morning</u>, as soon as I wake up, I pour myself a hot cup of coffee and read at least one chapter. Then, when I finish, I write down my impressions. I love to write. I <u>usually</u> make time to write in my journal <u>every day</u>. <u>Sometimes</u>, I write reflections. <u>Sometimes</u>, I write poems. <u>Sometimes</u>, I just write about my cat. I guess that makes me seem introverted, but I also can be very social. I have lots of friends. <u>Every weekend</u>, we do something together. <u>Sometimes</u>, we meet at the park and go for a hike. <u>Sometimes</u>, we meet at a restaurant and try a new dish. <u>Every now and then</u>, we drive to a different city and see the sights. <u>Occasionally</u>, my friends want to go to a night club. That gets me out of my comfort zone. Although I like music, I <u>almost never</u> dance. My Brazilian friends says that (if I learned the Samba, I would feel a lot more confident!) Hopefully, one day!

NOTES: Use this space to write notes about the usage of this tense.

---

bookworm: big reader

have my nose in a book: read intently

introverted: quiet and solitary

Every now and then: occasionally

out of my comfort zone: do something different

Samba: a Brazilian dance

Now you try! Write a paragraph in which you talk about your habits and hobbies. Use adverbs of frequency (always, sometimes, usually, never) and at least one conditional (condition and consequence).

Simple Present Tense

SENTENCES IN PRESENT TENSE

LEVEL I

The fluffy dog   always   barks loudly
_____ always _____.
     NP   VP

LEVEL II

The red rooster   crows noisily   every time   the sun   rises.
_____ _____ every time _____ _____.
    NP   VP   NP   VP

LEVEL III

The horse only gallops when she races in the summer?
_____ only _____ when _____ _____?
    NP   VP   NP   VP

Note: Practice Pages utilize the generative rules introduced in the introduction to students section to encourage students to make as creative sentences as possible.

Simple Sentence
S → NP VP

Verb Phrase:
VP → (Adv) V (NP) (NP) (PP) (Adv)
VP → (Adv) V (VP) (PP) (Adv)
Noun Phrase:
NP → (Art) (Adj*) N (RC) (PP)

Adv = Adverb: *always, often, quickly, suddenly*
PP = Prepositional Phrase: *in, on, from*
Art = Article: *a, an, the*
Adj = Adjectives: *cute, fluffy, white*
RC = Relative Clause: the cat *that I saw at the shelter*

Parentheses () means optional
Asterick * means can have multiple

Simple Present Tense

PRACTICE SENTENCES

1. _____
   _____
2. _____
   _____
3. _____
   _____

1. _____
   _____
2. _____
   _____
3. _____
   _____

1. _____
   _____
2. _____
   _____
3. _____
   _____

Notes: Use this space to note common mistakes, instances you can use the tense or anything that helps you use the tense.
Notes: Use this space to note common mistakes, instances you can use the tense or anything that helps you use the tense.

Simple Present Tense

QUESTIONS IN PRESENT TENSE

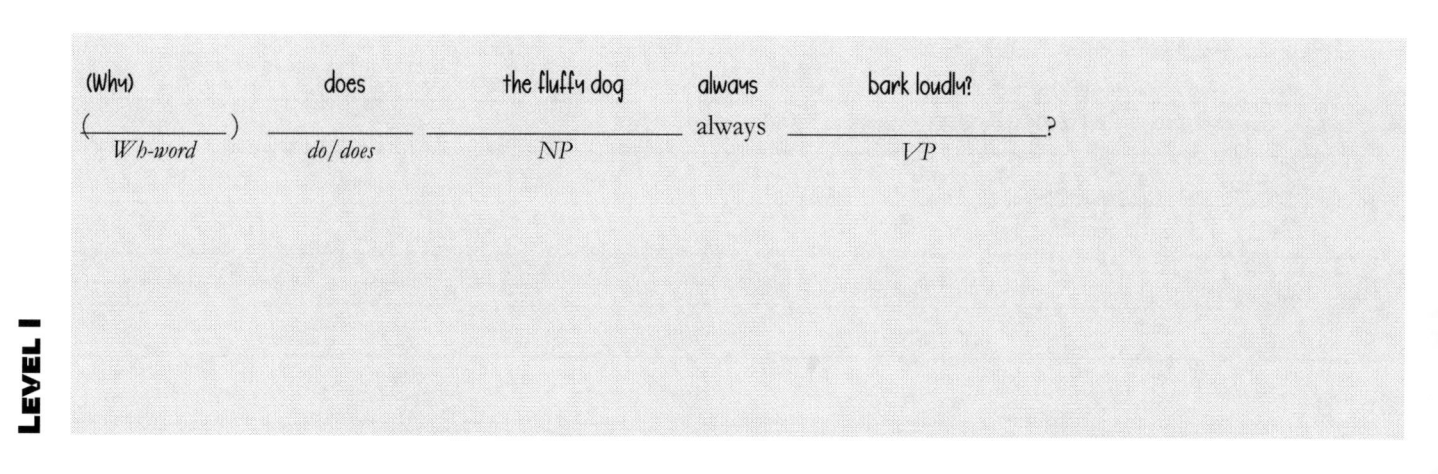

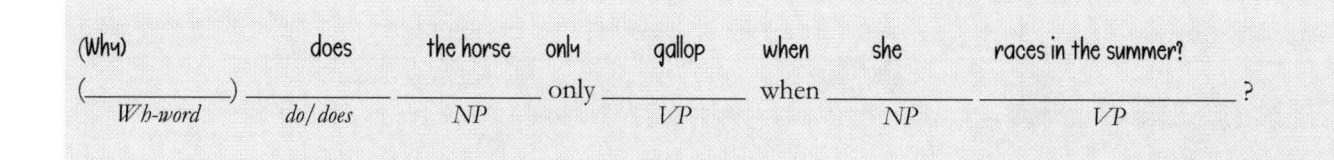

LEVEL I

(Why)   does   the fluffy dog   always   bark loudly?
(_____) _____ _____ always _____ ?
Wh-word   *do/does*   NP   VP

LEVEL II

(Why)   does   the red rooster   crow noisily   every time   the sun   rises?
(_____) _____ _____ _____ every time _____ _____ ?
Wh-word   *do/does*   NP   VP   NP   VP

LEVEL III

(Why)   does   the horse   only   gallop   when   she   races in the summer?
(_____) _____ _____ only _____ when _____ _____ ?
Wh-word   *do/does*   NP   VP   NP   VP

Note: Practice Pages utilize the generative rules introduced in the introduction to students section to encourage students to make as creative sentences as possible.

Simple Sentence
S → NP VP

Verb Phrase:
VP → (Adv) V (NP) (NP) (PP) (Adv)
VP → (Adv) V (VP) (PP) (Adv)

Noun Phrase:
NP → (Art) (Adj*) N (RC) (PP)

Adv = Adverb: *always, often, quickly, suddenly*
PP = Prepositional Phrase: *in, on, from*
Art = Article: *a, an, the*
Adj = Adjectives: *cute, fluffy, white*
RC = Relative Clause: the cat *that I saw at the shelter*

Parentheses () means optional
Asterick * means can have multiple

24

Simple Present Tense

PRACTICE SENTENCES

1. _____
   _____
2. _____
   _____
3. _____
   _____

1. _____
   _____
2. _____
   _____
3. _____
   _____

1. _____
   _____
2. _____
   _____
3. _____
   _____

Notes: Use this space to note common mistakes, instances you can use the tense or anything that helps you use the tense.
Notes: Use this space to note common mistakes, instances you can use the tense or anything that helps you use the tense.

Simple Present Tense

NEGATIVE STATEMENTS IN PRESENT TENSE

LEVEL I

The tiny dog   doesn't   always   bark.
_____ _____ always _____.
     NP   don't/doesn't   VP

LEVEL II

The rooster   doesn't   always   crow   every time   the sun   rises.
_____ _____ always _____ every time _____ _____.
     NP   don't/doesn't   VP   NP   VP

LEVEL III

The horse   doesn't   only   gallop fast   when   she   races in the summer.
_____ _____ only _____ when _____ _____.
    NP   don't/doesn't   VP   NP   VP

Note: Practice Pages utilize the generative rules introduced in the introduction to students section to encourage students to make as creative sentences as possible.

Simple Sentence
S → NP VP

Verb Phrase:
VP → (Adv) V (NP) (NP) (PP) (Adv)
VP → (Adv) V (VP) (PP) (Adv)

Noun Phrase:
NP → (Art) (Adj*) N (RC) (PP)

Adv = Adverb: *always, often, quickly, suddenly*
PP = Prepositional Phrase: *in, on, from*
Art = Article: *a, an, the*
Adj = Adjectives: *cute, fluffy, white*
RC = Relative Clause: the cat *that I saw at the shelter*

Parentheses () means optional
Asterick * means can have multiple

Simple Present Tense

PRACTICE SENTENCES

1. _____
   _____
2. _____
   _____
3. _____
   _____

1. _____
   _____
2. _____
   _____
3. _____
   _____

1. _____
   _____
2. _____
   _____
3. _____
   _____

Notes: Use this space to note common mistakes, instances you can use the tense or anything that helps you use the tense.
Notes: Use this space to note common mistakes, instances you can use the tense or anything that helps you use the tense.

Simple Present Tense

MODAL STATEMENTS IN PRESENT TENSE

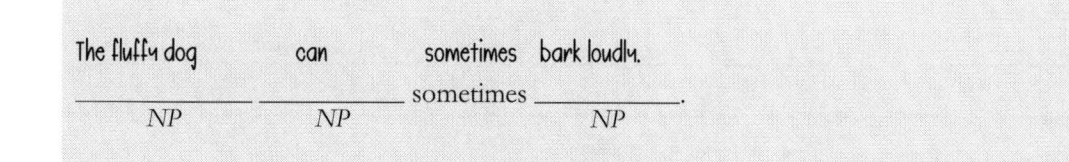

LEVEL I

The fluffy dog   can   sometimes bark loudly.

_____ _____ sometimes _____.
   NP   NP   NP

LEVEL II

The rooster   must   crow   every time   the sun   rises.

_____ _____ _____ every time _____ _____.
  NP   *modal*   VP   NP   VP

LEVEL III

The horse   can   only   gallop   when   she   races in the summer.

_____ _____ only _____ when _____ _____.
  NP   *modal*   VP   NP   VP

Note: Practice Pages utilize the generative rules introduced in the introduction to students section to encourage students to make as creative sentences as possible.

Simple Sentence
S → NP VP

Verb Phrase:
VP → (Adv) V (NP) (NP) (PP) (Adv)
VP → (Adv) V (VP) (PP) (Adv)

Noun Phrase:
NP → (Art) (Adj*) N (RC) (PP)

Adv = Adverb: *always, often, quickly, suddenly*
PP = Prepositional Phrase: *in, on, from*
Art = Article: *a, an, the*
Adj = Adjectives: *cute, fluffy, white*
RC = Relative Clause: the cat *that I saw at the shelter*

Parentheses () means optional
Asterick * means can have multiple

Simple Present Tense

PRACTICE SENTENCES

1. _____
_____
2. _____
_____
3. _____
_____

1. _____
_____
2. _____
_____
3. _____
_____

1. _____
_____
2. _____
_____
3. _____
_____

Notes: Use this space to note common mistakes, instances you can use the tense or anything that helps you use the tense.

Simple Present Tense

NOUN CLAUSES STATEMENTS IN PRESENT TENSE

LEVEL I

I know	why	the fluffy dog	always barks.
Introductory clause	wh-word	NP	VP

LEVEL II

I know	why	the rooster	crows	every time	the sun	rises
Introductory clause	wh-word	NP	VP	every time	NP	VP

LEVEL III

I know	why	the horse	only	gallops	when	she	races in the summer.
Introductory clause	wh-word	NP	only	VP	when	NP	VP

Note: Practice Pages utilize the generative rules introduced in the introduction to students section to encourage students to make as creative sentences as possible.

Simple Sentence
S → NP VP

Verb Phrase:
VP → (Adv) V (NP) (NP) (PP) (Adv)
VP → (Adv) V (VP) (PP) (Adv)

Noun Phrase:
NP → (Art) (Adj*) N (RC) (PP)

Adv = Adverb: *always, often, quickly, suddenly*
PP = Prepositional Phrase: *in, on, from*
Art = Article: *a, an, the*
Adj = Adjectives: *cute, fluffy, white*
RC = Relative Clause: the cat *that I saw at the shelter*

Parentheses () means optional
Asterick * means can have multiple

Simple Present Tense

PRACTICE SENTENCES

1. _____
   _____
2. _____
   _____
3. _____
   _____

1. _____
   _____
2. _____
   _____
3. _____
   _____

1. _____
   _____
2. _____
   _____
3. _____
   _____

Notes: Use this space to note common mistakes, instances you can use the tense or anything that helps you use the tense.

Present Progressive Tense

Rules

Simple progressive tense is a way of talking about what is happening **right now**.
I am working right now.

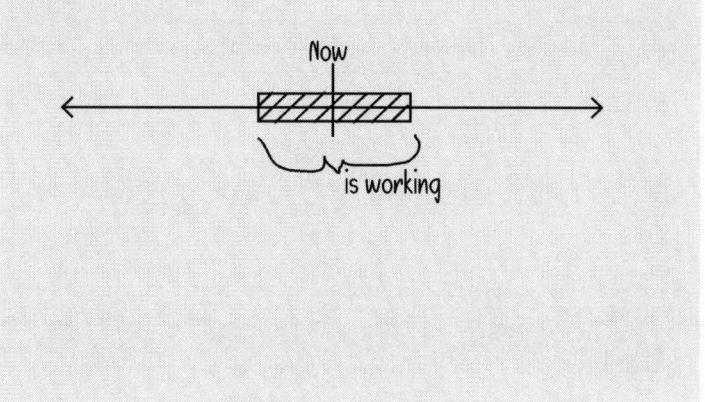

1.1 Warm Up

How many things can you think of that are happening right now?

In the classroom,

1. the clock is ticking.

2.

3.

At the beach,

1. the waves are breaking.

2.

3.

In the city,

1. horns are honking.

2.

3.

Present Progressive Tense Forms

I	am	working	right now.

He She It	is	working	

You We They	are	working	

Negative Present Progressive Tense Forms

I'm	not	working	right now.

He She It	isn't	working	

You We They	aren't	working	

Yes-No Qs Present Progressive Tense Forms

Am	I	working	right now?

Is	he she it	working	

Are	you we they	working	

Wh Qs Present Progressive Tense Forms

Where	am	I	working	right now?

Why	is	he she it	working	

Where	are	you we they	working	

Present Progressive Tense

Level I sentences

(One clause)

The adverb ("still") comes between "is" and the verb."

Level II sentences

Add a prepositional phrase. *In the noun, on the noun.*

The adverb of manner (*loudly*) comes **after** the verb.

Level III sentences

Add an additional prepositional phrase.

Level IV sentences

(Two parallel clauses linked with *while*).

1. The black cat is <u>purring</u>.

The _____ _____ is/are _____ .
     adjective   *noun(s)*   *is/are verbing obj*

2. The black cat is <u>still</u> purring.

The _____ _____ is/are still _____ .
     adjective   *noun(s)*   *is/are verbing obj*

3. The black cat is purring <u>on the carpet.</u>

The _____ _____ _____ _____ .
     adjective   *noun(s)*   *is/are verbing*   *prep phrase*

4. The black cat is <u>still</u> purring <u>loudly</u> on the carpet.

The _____ _____ is/are still _____ _____ .
     adjective   *noun(s)*   *verbing*   *adverb + prep phrase*

5. The black cat <u>with the white tail</u> is purring loudly on the carpet.

The _____ _____ with the _____ _____
     adjective   *noun(s)*   *adjective*   *noun(s)*

is/are _____ _____ .
    verbing   *adverb + prep phrase*

6. The black <u>cat</u> with the white tail <u>is</u> purring loudly <u>in the corner of the</u> carpet.

The _____ _____ with the _____ _____
     adjective   *noun(s)*   *adjective*   *noun(s)*

is/are _____ _____ .
    verbing   *adverb + prep phrase + prep phrase*

7. <u>While</u> the black cat is purring on the carpet, the angry dog is growling in the yard.

While _____ _____ _____ _____ ,
      adjective   *noun(s)*   *is/are verbing*   *prep phrase*

the _____ _____ _____ _____ .
    adjective   *noun(s)*   *is/are verbing*   *prep phrase*

Present Progressive Tense

LET'S ASK SOME QUESTIONS

Take a couple of your sentences from the previous page. Write four questions. Use the "yes/no" form or ""

Example:

Is the cat purring?
Why is the cat purring?

_____ _____ _____ _____
     BE   noun(s)   verb+ing   object

_____ _____ _____ _____
    Why BE   noun(s)   verb+ing   object

1. _____?
2. _____?
3. _____?
4. _____?

> Present progressive talks about what is happening *right now*. Questions often start with "to be" or "why."
>
> Examples:
>
> *Are you sleeping?*
>
> *Why is she yelling?*
>
> *Is the woman going home?*
>
> *Why are the cars driving so fast?*

NOW ANSWER WITH A NOUN CLAUSE

Pick one of the introductory clauses below:
It doesn't matter   I don't know   It's not important   It's not clear   I can't say

I don't know <u>whether or not</u> the cat is purring.
                    (if)
It doesn't matter <u>why</u> the cat is purring.

_____ _____ _____ _____
 Introductory clause   whether or not/ if/ why   noun(s)   BE verb+ing

Write four answers to the questions above using an introductory clause.

1. _____
2. _____
3. _____
4. _____

> Questions of the form, "Is she sleeping" are yes/no questions. When yes/no questions become noun-clauses they take *if* or *whether or not.*
>
> Examples:
>
> *I don't know if she's sleeping.*
>
> *It doesn't matter whether or not he's coming home.*
>
> *I can't say why the child's crying.*

Present Progressive Tense

CONDITIONS AND CONSEQUENCES

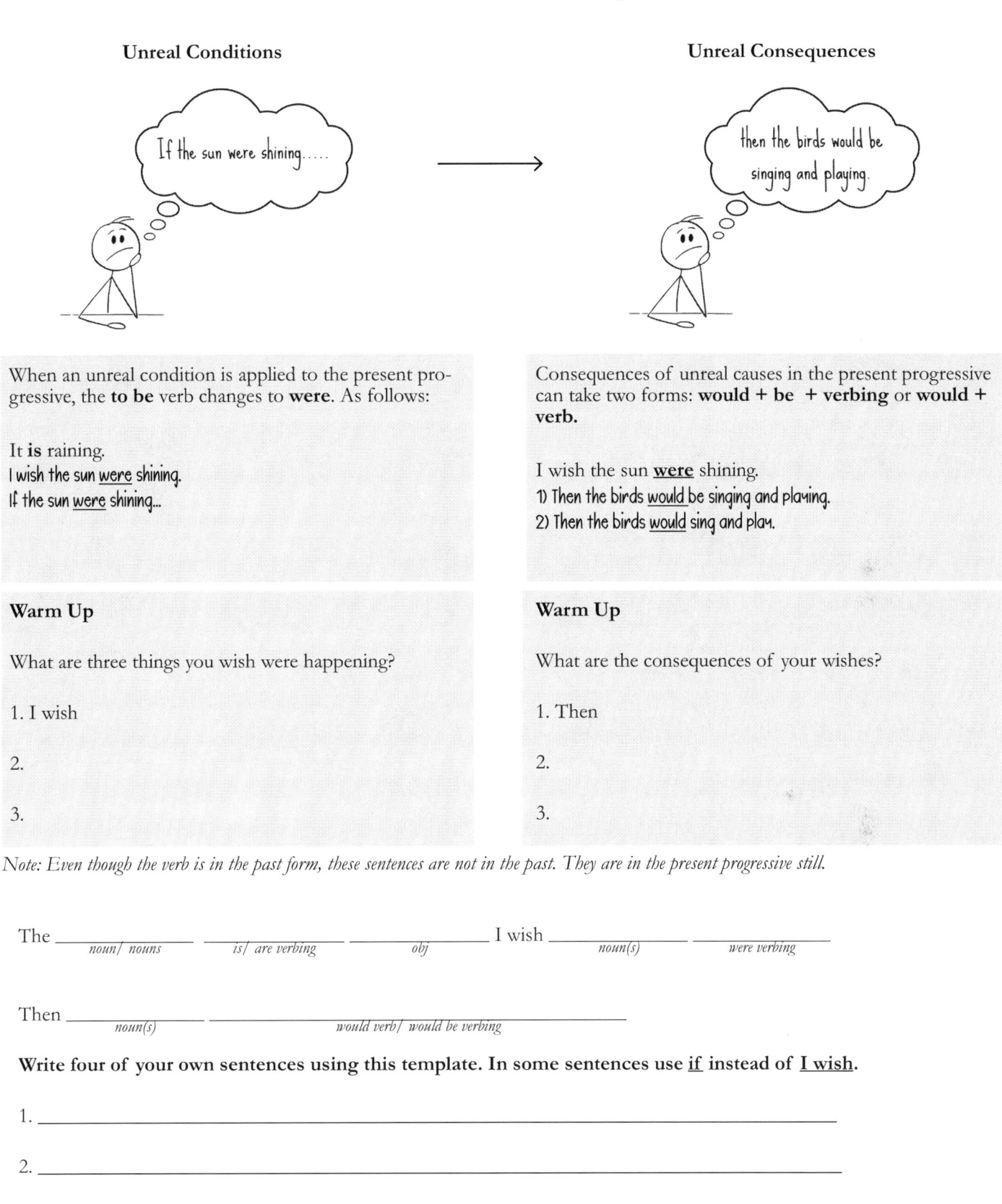

Unreal Conditions

If the sun were shining.....

→

Unreal Consequences

then the birds would be singing and playing.

When an unreal condition is applied to the present progressive, the **to be** verb changes to **were**. As follows:

It **is** raining.
I wish the sun were shining.
If the sun were shining...

Consequences of unreal causes in the present progressive can take two forms: **would + be + verbing** or **would + verb.**

I wish the sun **were** shining.
1) Then the birds would be singing and playing.
2) Then the birds would sing and play.

Warm Up

What are three things you wish were happening?

1. I wish

2.

3.

Warm Up

What are the consequences of your wishes?

1. Then

2.

3.

Note: Even though the verb is in the past form, these sentences are not in the past. They are in the present progressive still.

The _____ _____ _____ I wish _____ _____
   noun/ nouns   *is/ are verbing*   *obj*   *noun(s)*   *were verbing*

Then _____ _____
      noun(s)   *would verb/ would be verbing*

Write four of your own sentences using this template. In some sentences use <u>if</u> instead of <u>I wish</u>.

1. _____

2. _____

3. _____

4 _____

Present Progressive Tense

PRACTICAL APPLICATION

Read the following short paragraph. <u>Underline</u> the expressions of frequency. (Circle) the conditionals.

A Day At The Beach

It's a beautiful day at the beach. The sun is shining. The waves are **breaking** gently on the shore. Out past the swells, a couple of surfers are trying to **catch waves** as they come in. A girl with a **boogie board** is lying flat on her stomach, **paddling** out to deeper water. A school of dolphins is swimming. Their fins are **slicing** out of the water, and a crowd of **onlookers** is gathering around to take pictures. On the beach itself, everyone is having a good time. Children are building sand castles. Their parents are lying on blankets, tanning, or reading novels. One family has a puppy. The golden retreiver is jumping up and down in the shallow water, **yapping** and yapping. Since the sun is hot overhead, some people are taking shelter under umbrellas. One man is **struggling** to open his up. It keeps **tilting** over in the sand. On the opposite blanket, a young woman is playing lively **calypso** music on her great, big boombox. The sound of the music is mixing with the rush of the wind and the **crumping** of the water. Across the beach, on the boardwalk, a man at a concession stand is selling snow cones and **funnel cakes**. The seagulls are swarming and cawing. One keeps **divebombing** at a little girl's cake. She wishes the gulls were less aggressive!

NOTES:

---

breaking: splashing

catch waves: surf

boogie board: styrafoam surf board

paddling: rowing

slicing: cutting

onlooker: watcher

yapping: barking

struggling: fighting

tilting: leaning

calypso: island music

crumpling: wrinkling

funnel cake: sweet, dry cake common at beaches

Now you try! Write a paragraph in which you describe a scene in which multiple actions are in progress. What is happening?

Present Progressive Tense

SENTENCES IN PRESENT PROGRESSIVE TENSE

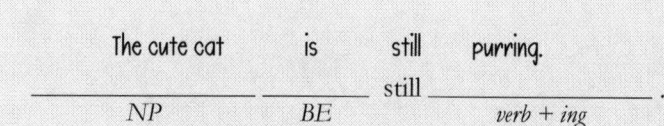

LEVEL I

The cute cat — is — still — purring.
_____ _____ still _____.
NP   BE   verb + ing

LEVEL II

The cute cat — is — still — purring — on the carpet.
_____ _____ still _____ _____.
NP   BE   verb + ing   PP

LEVEL III

The black cat — with the white tail — is — still — purring — on the carpet.
_____ _____ _____ still _____ _____.
NP   PP   BE   verb + ing   PP

Note: Practice Pages utilize the generative rules introduced in the introduction to students section to encourage students to make as creative sentences as possible.

Simple Sentence
S → NP VP

Verb Phrase:
VP → (Adv) V (NP) (NP) (PP) (Adv)
VP → (Adv) V (VP) (PP) (Adv)

Noun Phrase:
NP → (Art) (Adj*) N (RC) (PP)

Adv = Adverb: *always, often, quickly, suddenly*
PP = Prepositional Phrase: *in, on, from*
Art = Article: *a, an, the*
Adj = Adjectives: *cute, fluffy, white*
RC = Relative Clause: the cat *that I saw at the shelter*

Parentheses () means optional
Asterick * means can have multiple

Present Progressive Tense

PRACTICE SENTENCES

1. _____
2. _____
3. _____

1. _____
2. _____
3. _____

1. _____
2. _____
3. _____

Notes: Use this space to note common mistakes, instances you can use the tense or anything that helps you use the tense.

Present Progressive Tense

QUESTIONS IN PROGRESSIVE TENSE

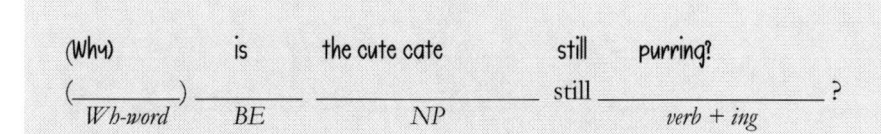

LEVEL I

(Why)   is   the cute cate   still   purring?

(_____) _____ _____ still _____ ?
Wh-word   *BE*   *NP*   *verb + ing*

LEVEL II

(Why)   is   the cute cate   still   purring   on the carpet ?

(_____) _____ _____ still _____ _____ ?
Wh-word   *BE*   *NP*   *verb + ing*   *PP*

LEVEL III

(Where)   is   the black cat   with the white tail   purring ?

(_____) _____ _____ _____ _____ ?
Wh-word   *BE*   *NP*   *PP*   *verb + ing*

Note: Practice Pages utilize the generative rules introduced in the introduction to students section to encourage students to make as creative sentences as possible.

Simple Sentence
S → NP VP

Verb Phrase:
VP → (Adv) V (NP) (NP) (PP) (Adv)
VP → (Adv) V (VP) (PP) (Adv)

Noun Phrase:
NP → (Art) (Adj*) N (RC) (PP)

Adv = Adverb: *always, often, quickly, suddenly*
PP = Prepositional Phrase: *in, on, from*
Art = Article: *a, an, the*
Adj = Adjectives: *cute, fluffy, white*
RC = Relative Clause: the cat *that I saw at the shelter*

Parentheses () means optional
Asterick * means can have multiple

Present Progressive Tense

PRACTICE SENTENCES

1. _____
_____
2. _____
_____
3. _____
_____

1. _____
_____
2. _____
_____
3. _____
_____

1. _____
_____
2. _____
_____
3. _____
_____

Notes: Use this space to note common mistakes, instances you can use the tense or anything that helps you use the tense.

Present Progressive Tense

NEGATIVE STATEMENTS IN PROGRESSIVE TENSE

LEVEL I

The cute cat	isn't	purring	anymore.
NP	isn't/aren't	verb + ing	anymore.

LEVEL II

The cute cat	isn't	purring	on the carpet	anymore.
NP	isn't/aren't	verb + ing	PP	anymore.

LEVEL III

The black cat	with the white tail	isn't	purring	on the carpet	anymore.
NP	PP	isn't/aren't	verb + ing	PP	anymore.

Note: Practice Pages utilize the generative rules introduced in the introduction to students section to encourage students to make as creative sentences as possible.

Simple Sentence
S → NP VP

Verb Phrase:
VP → (Adv) V (NP) (NP) (PP) (Adv)
VP → (Adv) V (VP) (PP) (Adv)

Noun Phrase:
NP → (Art) (Adj*) N (RC) (PP)

Adv = Adverb: *always, often, quickly, suddenly*
PP = Prepositional Phrase: *in, on, from*
Art = Article: *a, an, the*
Adj = Adjectives: *cute, fluffy, white*
RC = Relative Clause: the cat *that I saw at the shelter*

Parentheses () means optional
Asterick * means can have multiple

Present Progressive Tense

PRACTICE SENTENCES

1. _____
_____
2. _____
_____
3. _____
_____

1. _____
_____
2. _____
_____
3. _____
_____

1. _____
_____
2. _____
_____
3. _____
_____

Notes: Use this space to note common mistakes, instances you can use the tense or anything that helps you use the tense.

Present Progressive Tense

MODAL STATEMENTS IN PROGRESSIVE TENSE

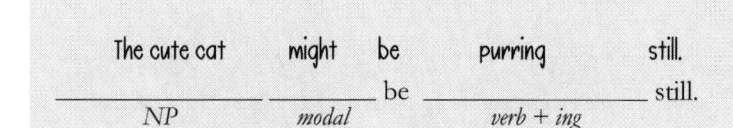

LEVEL I

The cute cat — might — be — purring — still.
_____ _____ be _____ still.
NP   modal   verb + ing

LEVEL II

The cute cat — might — still be — purring — on the carpet.
_____ _____ still be _____ _____.
NP   modal   verb + ing   PP

LEVEL III

The cute cat — with the white tail — might — still be — purring — on the carpet.
_____ _____ _____ still be _____ _____.
NP   PP   modal   verb + ing   PP

Note: Practice Pages utilize the generative rules introduced in the introduction to students section to encourage students to make as creative sentences as possible.

Simple Sentence
S → NP VP

Verb Phrase:
VP → (Adv) V (NP) (NP) (PP) (Adv)
VP → (Adv) V (VP) (PP) (Adv)

Noun Phrase:
NP → (Art) (Adj*) N (RC) (PP)

Adv = Adverb: *always, often, quickly, suddenly*
PP = Prepositional Phrase: *in, on, from*
Art = Article: *a, an, the*
Adj = Adjectives: *cute, fluffy, white*
RC = Relative Clause: the cat *that I saw at the shelter*

Parentheses () means optional
Asterick * means can have multiple

Present Progressive Tense

PRACTICE SENTENCES

1. _____
_____
2. _____
_____
3. _____
_____

1. _____
_____
2. _____
_____
3. _____
_____

1. _____
_____
2. _____
_____
3. _____
_____

Notes: Use this space to note common mistakes, instances you can use the tense or anything that helps you use the tense.

Present Progressive Tense

NOUN CLAUSES STATEMENTS IN PROGRESSIVE TENSE

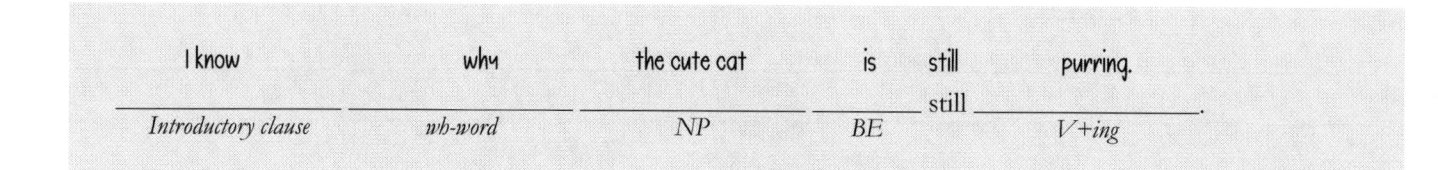

LEVEL I

I know	why	the cute cat	is	still	purring.
Introductory clause	wh-word	NP	BE	still	V+ing

LEVEL II

I know	why	the cute cat	is	still	purring	on the carpet.
Introductory clause	wh-word	NP	BE	still	V+ing	PP

LEVEL III

I know	why	the cute cat	with the white tail	is	still	purring	on the carpet.
Introductory clause	wh-word	NP	PP	BE	still	V+ing	PP

Note: Practice Pages utilize the generative rules introduced in the introduction to students section to encourage students to make as creative sentences as possible.

Simple Sentence
S → NP VP

Verb Phrase:
VP → (Adv) V (NP) (NP) (PP) (Adv)
VP → (Adv) V (VP) (PP) (Adv)

Noun Phrase:
NP → (Art) (Adj*) N (RC) (PP)

Adv = Adverb: *always, often, quickly, suddenly*
PP = Prepositional Phrase: *in, on, from*
Art = Article: *a, an, the*
Adj = Adjectives: *cute, fluffy, white*
RC = Relative Clause: the cat *that I saw at the shelter*

Parentheses () means optional
Asterick * means can have multiple

Present Progressive Tense

PRACTICE SENTENCES

1. _____
2. _____
3. _____

1. _____
2. _____
3. _____

1. _____
2. _____
3. _____

Notes: Use this space to note common mistakes, instances you can use the tense or anything that helps you use the tense.

Simple Past Tense

Rules

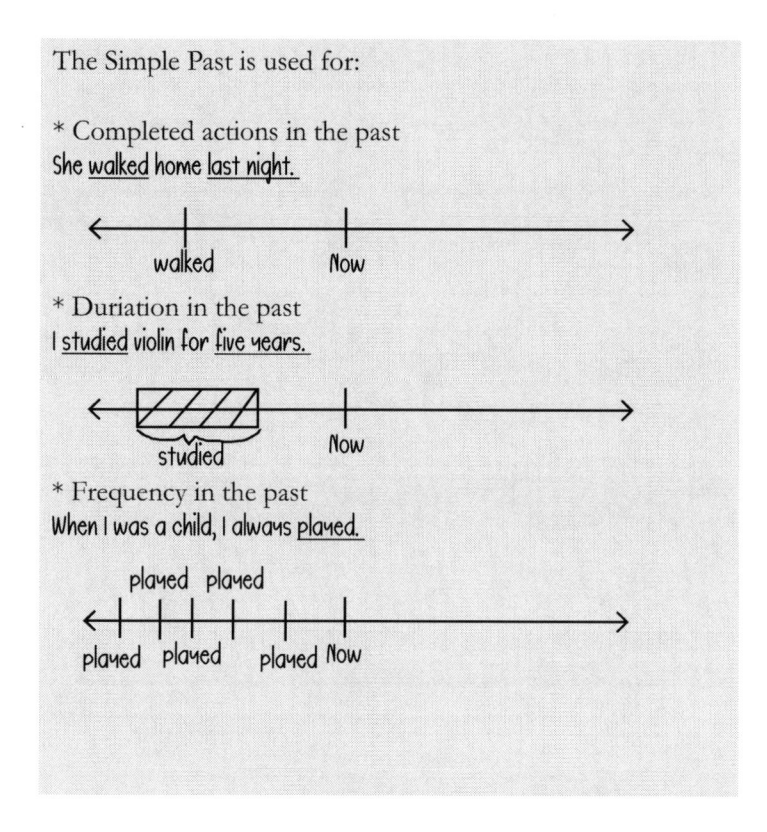

The Simple Past is used for:

* Completed actions in the past
She walked home last night.

```
←————|————————|————————→
    walked          Now
```

* Duration in the past
I studied violin for five years.

```
←——[////]————|————————→
    studied      Now
```

* Frequency in the past
When I was a child, I always played.

```
   played  played
←——|——|——|——|————————→
 played played played Now
```

1.1 Warm Up

Yesterday,

1. I studied English.

2.

3.

When I was a child,

1. I played football.

2.

3.

Last weekend,

1. my friend visited me.

2.

3

Simple Past Tense Forms

I		worked	yesterday.
He She It		worked	
You We They		worked	

Negative Past Tense Forms

I	didn't	work	yesterday.
He She It	didn't	work	
You We They	didn't	work	

Yes-No Qs Past Tense Forms

Did	I	work	yesterday?
Did	he she it	work	
Did	you we they	work	

Wh Qs Past Tense Forms

Where	did	I	work	yesterday?
Why	did	he she it	work	
Where	did	you we they	work	

Simple Past Tense

Level I sentences

Specific time (*At 1:00 this morning, last night*) and one clause.

1. <u>Yesterday</u>, the brown horse <u>galloped.</u>

   _____ the _____ _____ _____.
   Time word   *adjective*   *noun(s)*   *verbed +obj*

2. **The brown horse galloped <u>yesterday.</u>**

   The _____ _____ _____ _____.
        adjective   *noun(s)*   *verbed +obj*   *time word*

Level II sentences

Add a "for" phrase.

3. **Yesterday, the brown horse galloped <u>for an hour</u>.**

   _____ the _____ _____ _____ _____.
   time word   *adjective*   *noun(s)*   *verbed +obj*   *for + time*

4. **The brown horse galloped for an hour <u>yesterday</u>.**

   The _____ _____ _____ _____ _____.
        adjective   *noun(s)*   *verbed +obj*   *for+ time*   *time word*

Level III sentences

Add an additional prepositional phrase.

Add multiple, parallel verbs.

5. **The brown horse <u>with its powerful muscles</u> galloped for an hour yesterday.**

   The _____ _____ with the _____ _____
        adjective   *noun(s)*   *adjective*   *noun(s)*

   _____ _____.
   verbed + obj   *for + time + time word*

Level IV sentences

Add as second clause.

Note position of adverb.

6. **The brown horse, <u>snorted</u>, <u>neighed</u>, and <u>galloped</u>.**

   The _____ _____ _____ _____ _____.
        adjective   *noun(s)*   *verbed +obj*   *verbed + obj*   *and verbed+ obj*

7. **Yesterday, <u>when the sun rose</u>, the black horse snorted, neighed, and galloped.**

   _____ when _____ _____, _____ _____
   time word   *noun(s)*   *verbed*   *adjective*   *noun(s)*

   _____, _____ and _____
   verbed + obj   *verbed + obj*   *verbed +obj*

Simple Past Tense

LET'S ASK SOME QUESTIONS

Take a couple of your sentences from the previous page. Write four questions. Use the "yes/no" form or a "wh-word"

Example:

Did the horse gallop?
Where did the horse gallop?

_____ _____ _____ _____
    Did   noun(s)   verb+ing   object

_____ _____ _____ _____
  Wh-word did   noun(s)   verb+ing   object

1. _____?

2. _____?

3. _____?

4. _____?

> The simple past talks about finished actions in the past. It is used in a wide variety of questions.
>
> Examples:
>
> *Did you leave?*
>
> *When did they arrive?*
>
> *How did they do that?*
>
> *Who did she give the letter to?*
>
> *Where did they put the book?*

NOW ANSWER WITH A NOUN CLAUSE

Pick one of the introductory clauses below:
It doesn't matter   I don't know   It's not important   It's not clear   I can't say

I don't know <u>whether or not</u> the horse galloped.
             (if)
It doesn't matter <u>where</u> the horse galloped.

_____ _____ _____ _____
 Introductory clause   whethe or notr/ if/ wh-word   noun(s)   verbed

Write four answers to the questions above using an introductory clause.

1. _____

2. _____

3. _____

4. _____

> Questions of the form, "Did you sleep" are yes/no questions. When yes/no questions become noun-clauses they take *if* or *whether or not.*
>
> Examples:
>
> *I don't know if she slept.*
>
> *It doesn't matter whether or not he came home.*
>
> *I can't say why the child cried.*

Simple Past Tense

CONDITIONS AND CONSEQUENCES

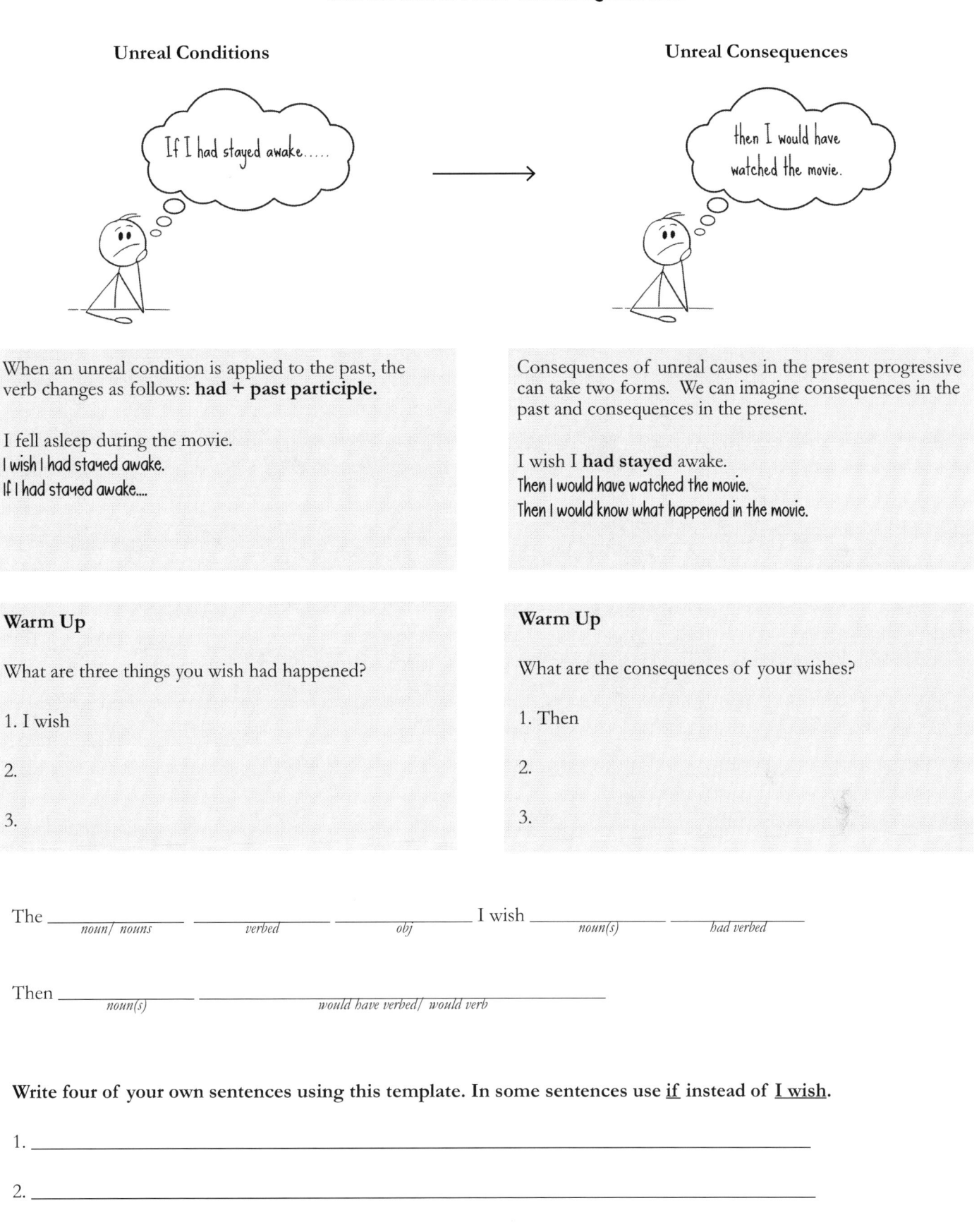

Unreal Conditions

If I had stayed awake......

→

Unreal Consequences

then I would have watched the movie.

When an unreal condition is applied to the past, the verb changes as follows: **had + past participle.**

I fell asleep during the movie.
I wish I had stayed awake.
If I had stayed awake....

Consequences of unreal causes in the present progressive can take two forms. We can imagine consequences in the past and consequences in the present.

I wish I **had stayed** awake.
Then I would have watched the movie.
Then I would know what happened in the movie.

Warm Up

What are three things you wish had happened?

1. I wish

2.

3.

Warm Up

What are the consequences of your wishes?

1. Then

2.

3.

The _____ _____ _____ I wish _____ _____
   noun/ nouns   *verbed*   *obj*   *noun(s)*   *had verbed*

Then _____ _____
      noun(s)   *would have verbed/ would verb*

Write four of your own sentences using this template. In some sentences use <u>if</u> instead of <u>I wish</u>.

1. _____

2. _____

3. _____

4 _____

Simple Past Tense

PRACTICAL APPLICATION

Read the following short paragraph. Underline the time words. Circle the conditionals.

Last Week

We had a great vacation in New York. On Sunday we landed at JFK Airport. We gathered our luggage, took an Uber into the city, and checked into our **Airbnb**. Since it was already late and we were **jetlagged**, we decided to just have a quick dinner and head to bed early. I wish we had felt livelier. Then we would have **hit the town**. On Monday, we got up early to see the sights. We took the metro downtown and went to the **Met**. Then we **circled around** to Central Park, **meandered** along the walking paths and **people-watched**. On Tuesday, we went to Times Square and hunted for celebrities. We didn't see anybody, but we took lots of selfies. On Wednesday, we were in a **bohemian** mood, so we visited **Greenwich Village** and learned about the famous **beat** writers and **avant garde** aritsts that lived there in the 60's. When Thursday **rolled around**, we wanted to do something **off the beaten path**, so we took the train up to the **Cloisters**. All the old Gothic art was beautiful. We took hundreds of pictures and wandered the grounds of the old monastery. Unfortunately, our flight home was on Friday. We had a quick bite to eat in the morning, took one more walk, and then ubered over to the airport. I really wish we had had more time to stay. With another week, we would have seen so many more things!

NOTES: Use this space to write notes about the usage of this tense.

Airbnb: rented rooms

jetlagged: tired from a flight

hit the town: visited the town

Met: famous museum in NYC

circle around: return

meander: wander

people-watch: look at people

bohemian: artistic

Greenwich village: historic NYC neighborhood

beat: style of poetry

avant garde: expirmental

roll around: return

off the beaten path: out of the way

Cloisters: museum in norther NYC.

Now you try! Write a paragraph in which you describe a week in the past. What happened on Monday, Tuesday, Wednesday, Thursday, and Friday?

Simple Past Tense

SENTENCES IN SIMPLE PAST

LEVEL I

```
   The horse         galloped        yesterday.
_____ _____ _____.
       NP            VP+past tense     Time Word
```

LEVEL II

```
   The horse         galloped    for   an hour        yesterday.
_____ _____for_____ _____.
       NP            VP+past tense    Time Duration     Time Word
```

LEVEL III

```
   The horse       galloped   and   trotted    for   an hour       yesterday.
_____ _____and_____for_____ _____.
      NP         VP+past tense       VP+past tense     Time Duration   Time Word
```

Note: Practice Pages utilize the generative rules introduced in the introduction to students section to encourage students to make as creative sentences as possible.

Simple Sentence
S → NP VP

Verb Phrase:
VP → (Adv) V (NP) (NP) (PP) (Adv)
VP → (Adv) V (VP) (PP) (Adv)

Noun Phrase:
NP → (Art) (Adj*) N (RC) (PP)

Adv = Adverb: *always, often, quickly, suddenly*
PP = Prepositional Phrase: *in, on, from*
Art = Article: *a, an, the*
Adj = Adjectives: *cute, fluffy, white*
RC = Relative Clause: the cat *that I saw at the shelter*

Parentheses () means optional
Asterick * means can have multiple

Simple Past Tense

PRACTICE SENTENCES

1. _____
   _____
2. _____
   _____
3. _____
   _____

1. _____
   _____
2. _____
   _____
3. _____
   _____

1. _____
   _____
2. _____
   _____
3. _____
   _____

Notes: Use this space to note common mistakes, instances you can use the tense or anything that helps you use the tense.

Simple Past Tense

QUESTIONS IN SIMPLE PAST TENSE

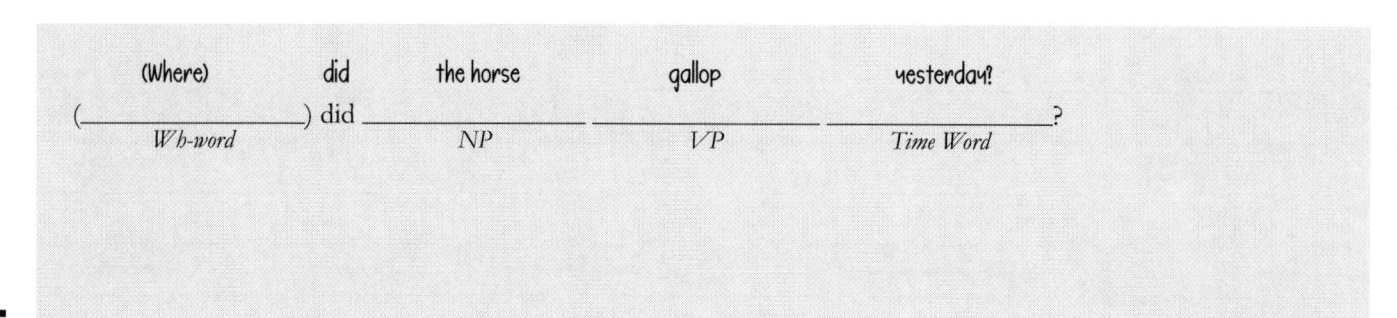

LEVEL I

(Where)   did   the horse   gallop   yesterday?

(_____) did _____ _____ _____?
   Wh-word   NP   VP   Time Word

LEVEL II

(Where)   did   the horse   gallop   for   an hour   yesterday?

(_____) did _____ _____ for _____ _____?
   Wh-word   NP   VP   Time Duration   Time Word

LEVEL III

(Where)   did   the horse   gallop   and   trot   for   an hour   yesterday?

(_____) did _____ _____ and _____ for _____ _____?
   Wh-word   NP   VP   VP   Time Duration   Time Word

Note: Practice Pages utilize the generative rules introduced in the introduction to students section to encourage students to make as creative sentences as possible.

Simple Sentence
S → NP VP

Verb Phrase:
VP → (Adv) V (NP) (NP) (PP) (Adv)
VP → (Adv) V (VP) (PP) (Adv)

Noun Phrase:
NP → (Art) (Adj*) N (RC) (PP)

Adv = Adverb: *always, often, quickly, suddenly*
PP = Prepositional Phrase: *in, on, from*
Art = Article: *a, an, the*
Adj = Adjectives: *cute, fluffy, white*
RC = Relative Clause: the cat *that I saw at the shelter*

Parentheses () means optional
Asterick * means can have multiple

Simple Past Tense

PRACTICE SENTENCES

1. _____
_____
2. _____
_____
3. _____
_____

1. _____
_____
2. _____
_____
3. _____
_____

1. _____
_____
2. _____
_____
3. _____
_____

Notes: Use this space to note common mistakes, instances you can use the tense or anything that helps you use the tense.

Simple Past Tense

NEGATIVE STATEMENTS IN SIMPLE PAST TENSE

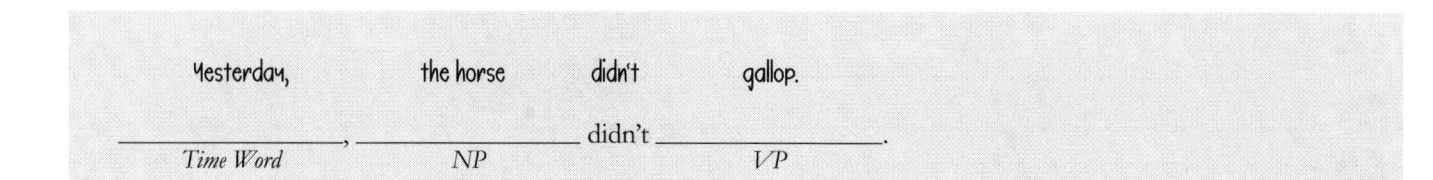

LEVEL I

Yesterday, the horse didn't gallop.

_____ , _____ didn't _____ .
Time Word   *NP*   *VP*

LEVEL II

Yesterday, the horse didn't gallop for an hour.

_____ , _____ didn't _____ for _____ .
Time Word   *NP*   *VP*   *Time*

LEVEL III

Yesterday, the horse didn't trot or gallop for an hour.

_____ , _____ didn't _____ or _____ for _____ .
Time Word   *NP*   *VP*   *VP*   *Time*

Note: Practice Pages utilize the generative rules introduced in the introduction to students section to encourage students to make as creative sentences as possible.

Simple Sentence
S → NP VP

Verb Phrase:
VP → (Adv) V (NP) (NP) (PP) (Adv)
VP → (Adv) V (VP) (PP) (Adv)

Noun Phrase:
NP → (Art) (Adj*) N (RC) (PP)

Adv = Adverb: *always, often, quickly, suddenly*
PP = Prepositional Phrase: *in, on, from*
Art = Article: *a, an, the*
Adj = Adjectives: *cute, fluffy, white*
RC = Relative Clause: the cat *that I saw at the shelter*

Parentheses () means optional
Asterick * means can have multiple

Simple Past Tense

PRACTICE SENTENCES

1. _____
   _____
2. _____
   _____
3. _____
   _____

1. _____
   _____
2. _____
   _____
3. _____
   _____

1. _____
   _____
2. _____
   _____
3. _____
   _____

Notes: Use this space to note common mistakes, instances you can use the tense or anything that helps you use the tense.

MODAL STATEMENTS IN SIMPLE PAST TENSE

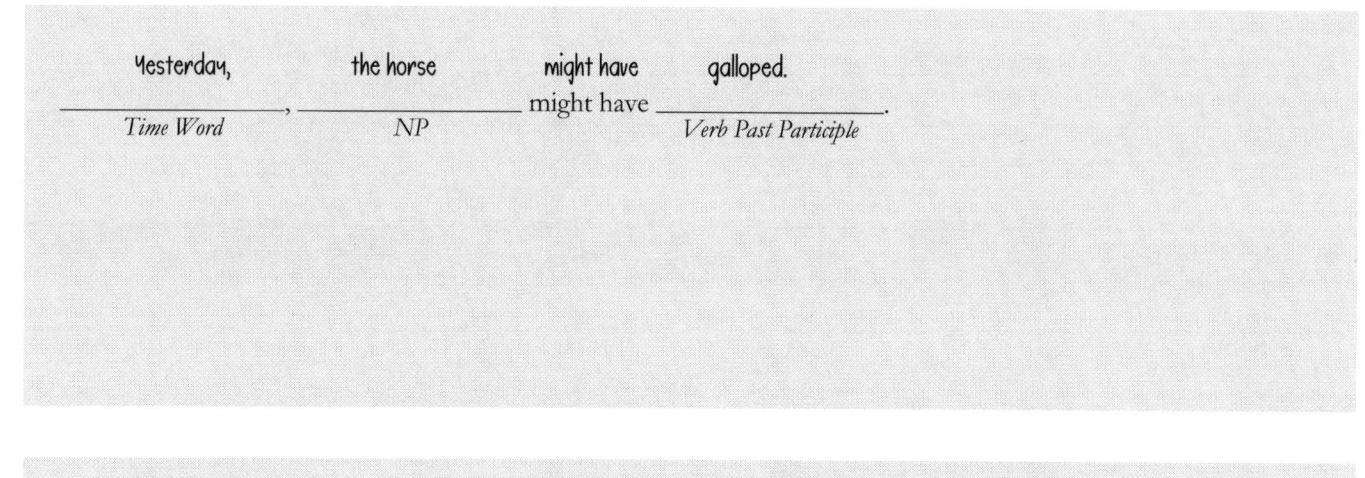

LEVEL I

Yesterday, the horse might have galloped.
_____, _____ might have _____.
Time Word   NP   Verb Past Participle

LEVEL II

Yesterday, the horse might have galloped for an hour.
_____, _____ might have _____ for _____.
Time Word   NP   Verb Past Participle   Time

LEVEL III

Yesterday, the horse might have galloped or trotted for an hour.
_____, _____ might have _____ or _____ for _____.
Time Word   NP   Verb Past Participle   Verb Past Participle   Time

---

Note: Practice Pages utilize the generative rules introduced in the introduction to students section to encourage students to make as creative sentences as possible.

Simple Sentence
S → NP VP

Verb Phrase:
VP → (Adv) V (NP) (NP) (PP) (Adv)
VP → (Adv) V (VP) (PP) (Adv)

Noun Phrase:
NP → (Art) (Adj*) N (RC) (PP)

Adv = Adverb: *always, often, quickly, suddenly*
PP = Prepositional Phrase: *in, on, from*
Art = Article: *a, an, the*
Adj = Adjectives: *cute, fluffy, white*
RC = Relative Clause: the cat *that I saw at the shelter*

Parentheses () means optional
Asterick * means can have multiple

Simple Past Tense

PRACTICE SENTENCES

1. _____
_____
2. _____
_____
3. _____
_____

1. _____
_____
2. _____
_____
3. _____
_____

1. _____
_____
2. _____
_____
3. _____
_____

Notes: Use this space to note common mistakes, instances you can use the tense or anything that helps you use the tense.

Simple Past Tense

NOUN CLAUSES STATEMENTS IN SIMPLE PAST TENSE

LEVEL I

I know	why	the horse	galloped	yesterday.
Introductory clause	*Wh-word*	*NP*	*Verb+ed*	*Time Word*

LEVEL II

I know	why	the horse	galloped	for	an hour	yesterday.
Introductory clause	*Wh-word*	*NP*	*Verb+ed*	for	*Time*	*Time Word*

LEVEL III

I know	why	the horse	galloped	and	trotted	for	an hour	yesterday.
Introductory clause	*Wh-word*	*NP*	*Verb+ed*	and	*Verb+ed*	for	*Time*	*Time Word*

Note: Practice Pages utilize the generative rules introduced in the introduction to students section to encourage students to make as creative sentences as possible.

Simple Sentence
S → NP VP

Verb Phrase:
VP → (Adv) V (NP) (NP) (PP) (Adv)
VP → (Adv) V (VP) (PP) (Adv)

Noun Phrase:
NP → (Art) (Adj*) N (RC) (PP)

Adv = Adverb: *always, often, quickly, suddenly*
PP = Prepositional Phrase: *in, on, from*
Art = Article: *a, an, the*
Adj = Adjectives: *cute, fluffy, white*
RC = Relative Clause: the cat *that I saw at the shelter*

Parentheses () means optional
Asterick * means can have multiple

Simple Past Tense

PRACTICE SENTENCES

1. _____
   _____
2. _____
   _____
3. _____
   _____

1. _____
   _____
2. _____
   _____
3. _____
   _____

1. _____
   _____
2. _____
   _____
3. _____
   _____

Notes: Use this space to note common mistakes, instances you can use the tense or anything that helps you use the tense.

Past Progressive Tense

Rules

The past progressive is used for:

* **Actions in progress at a specific time in the past**
At 1:00 yesterday, the birds were singing.

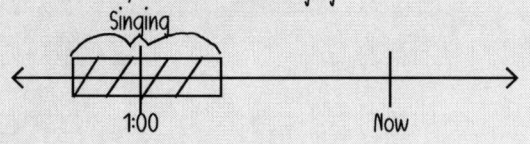

* **Actions interrupted in the past**
The phone rang when I was sleeping.

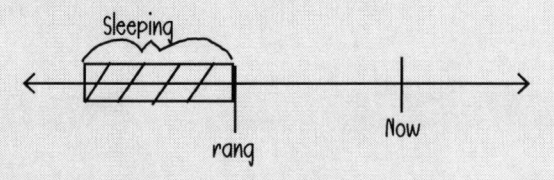

* **Simultaneous actions in the past**
While the sun was shining, the birds were singing.

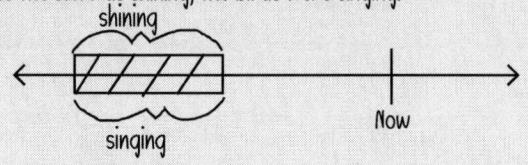

I.I Warm Up

What was happening yesterday at 8:00?

1. At 8:00, it was raining

2.

3.

What were you doing when the phone rang?

1. I was reading when the phone rang.

2.

3.

What were your friends and family doing at this time yesterday?

1. My brother was studying. My father...

2.

Past Progressive Tense Forms

I	was	working	yesterday
He She It	was	working	
You We They	were	working	

Negative Past Progressive Tense Forms

I	wasn't	working	yesterday
He She It	wasn't	working	
You We They	weren't	working	

Yes-No Qs Past Progressive Tense Forms

Was	I	working	yesterday?
Was	he she it	working	
Were	you we they	working	

Wh Qs Present Tense Forms

Where	was	I	working	yesterday?
Why	was	he she it	working	
Where	were	you we they	working	

Past Progressive Tense

Level I sentences

Time word (*Yesterday, this morning, last night*) and one clause.

Add an object

1. <u>At 1:00,</u> the pretty bird was singing.

_____ the _____ _____.
Specific time   *adjective*   *was verbing*

2. <u>At 1:00,</u> the pretty bird was singing <u>a cheerful song</u>.

_____ the _____ _____ _____.
specific time   *adj noun*   *was verbing*   *object*

Level II sentences

Simultaneous action, linked with "while"

3. <u>While</u> the pretty bird was singing a cheerful song, the worm was hiding.

While the _____ _____ _____ _____
     adjective   *noun*   *was verbing*   *obj*

_____ _____ _____.
adj noun   *was verbing*   *object*

Level III sentences

Add an interruption in the simple past.

Add multiple, parralel verbs.

4. The pretty bird was singing a cheerful song, <u>when suddenly</u>, the slender branch broke.

The _____ _____ _____ _____ when suddenly
   adjective   *noun(s)*   *was verbing*   *object*

_____ _____.
adj noun   *verbed + obj*

Level IV sentences

Add as second clause.

5. The sun was shining and the pretty bird was singing a cheerful song when suddenly the wind blew and the slender branch broke.

The _____ _____ _____ _____
   adjective   *noun(s)*   *was verbing*   *object*

and the _____ _____ _____ _____ when suddenly
     adjective   *noun(s)*   *was verbing*   *object*

the _____ _____ and the _____ _____.
  adj noun   *verbed + obj*   *adj noun*   *verbed + obj*

Past Progressive Tense

LET'S ASK SOME QUESTIONS

Take a couple of your sentences from the previous page. Write four questions. Use the "yes/no" form or a "wh-word"

Example:

Was the bird singing?
Why was the bird singing?

_____ _____ _____ _____
Was/Were   noun(s)   verb+ing   object

_____ _____ _____ _____ _____
Wh-word   Was/Were   noun(s)   verb+ing   object

1. _____?
2. _____?
3. _____?
4. _____?

> Past progressive talks about what was in progress (unfinished) at a moment in the past. Questions often start with "to be" or "why."
>
> Examples:
>
> *Were you sleeping when I called?*
>
> *Why was she crying so much yesterday?*
>
> *Was the woman trying to work at 12:00?*

NOW ANSWER WITH A NOUN CLAUSE

> Pick one of the introductory clauses below:
>
> It doesn't matter   I don't know   It's not important   It's not clear   I can't say

I don't know <u>whether or not</u> the bird was singing.
           (if)
It doesn't matter <u>why</u> the cat was singing.

_____ _____ _____ _____
Introductory clause   whether or not/ if/ why   noun(s)   is/are verbing

Write four answers to the questions above using an introductory clause.

1. _____
2. _____
3. _____
4. _____

> Questions of the form, "Was she sleeping" are yes/no questions. When yes/no questions become noun-clauses they take *if* or *whether or not.*
>
> Examples:
>
> *I don't know if she was sleeping.*
>
> *It doesn't matter whether or not he was coming home.*
>
> *I can't say why the child was crying.*

Past Progressive Tense

CONDITIONS AND CONSEQUENCES

Unreal Conditions

If the sun had been shining...

Unreal Consequences

then the birds would have been singing and playing.

When an unreal condition is applied to the past progressive, the "to be" verb changes to "had been." As follows:

It **was** raining yesterday.
I wish the sun had been shining.
If the sun had been shining...

Consequences of unreal causes in the present progressive can take two forms. We can imagine consequences in the past and consequences in the present.

I wish the sun had been shining.
Present: Then the birds would have been singing and playing.
Past: Then there wouldn't be puddles of water everywhere.

Warm Up

What are three things you wish had happened?

1. I wish

2.

3.

Warm Up

What are the consequences of your wishes?

1. Then

2.

3.

The _____ _____ _____ I wish _____ _____
     noun/ nouns   is/ are verbing   obj   noun(s)   were verbing

Then _____ _____
      noun(s)   would verb/ would be verbing

Write four of your own sentences using this template. In some sentences use <u>if</u> instead of <u>I wish</u>.

1. _____

2. _____

3. _____

4. _____

67

Past Progressive Tense

PRACTICAL APPLICATION

Read the following short paragraph. <u>Underline</u> vebs with -ing.

Interruption after Interruption!

When I got home yesterday, I just wanted to relax. It was 5:00 pm. Outside, it was **drizzling** gently. The rain was **ticking** in the trees, **tickling** their leaves. The house was quiet and peaceful. Nobody was stirring. My wife was doing yoga in the living room. My little daughter was asleep in her crib. The cat was **sleeping** on a big pile of cushions. The only one moving was the fish. I watched him swimming back and forth and back and forth. "You're a good friend," I said. "You don't make any noise." I went upstairs, grabbed my novel, filled up the tub, and **plopped** down in the bubbles. "Ah!" I said, "There's nothing like a hot bath after a long day." I stretched out my feet, opened my book, and started to read. I was just getting into the **plot** when I heard a knock at the door. "Wife!" I said, "Dear wife! Could you get the door? I'm in the bath." No answer. Sigh. I got out of the bath, dried off, pulled on some clothes and **jogged** downstairs. But when I got to the door, no one was there. "Huh!" I said, "What was that sound I heard?" I shrugged, went back upstairs, and climbed in the tub again. Once again, I was **just starting** to get absorbed in my book, when--bang! bang! bang!--I heard more knocking! This time, it sounded like it was coming from the living room. I ran downstairs and what did I see? The cat was **perched** on the counter, knocking at the aquarium glass with her paw! The fish was **whipping** back and forth, **lashing** his tail very frantically. "Hey!" I said, "Leave my friend alone!" I picked up the cat and **shooed** him away. "Goodness!" I said, "I wish you were more civilized!" I turned around and was just starting to climb the steps back to the tub, when the living room door swung open. It was my wife. "Honey," she said, "Did you hear a noise?"

NOTES: Use this space to write notes on the usage of the tense.

---

drizzle: slight rain

ticking: make a "tick" sound

tickling: gently brush

curl up: sleep like a cat

plop: sound of something landing in water

plot: story

jog: gentle run

just start: begin to do something. Takes the infinitive.

perched: to sit like a bird or a cat

whip: to go back and forth fast

lash: whip back and forth

shoo: to make go away

Now you try! Write a paragraph in which you describe a scene in which multiple actions are in progress in the past when an interruption happens.

Past Progressive Tense

SENTENCES IN PAST PROGRESSIVE TENSE

LEVEL I

The pretty bird — was — singing — at 1:00pm.
_____ _____ _____ at _____.
    NP   was/were   V+ing   Time

LEVEL II

The pretty bird — was — singing — while — the worm — was — hiding.
_____ _____ _____ while _____ _____ _____.
    NP   was/were   V+ing   NP   was/were   V+ing

LEVEL III

The pretty bird — was — singing — when suddenly — the slender branch — broke.
_____ _____ _____ when suddenly _____ _____.
    NP   was/were   V+ing   NP   V+simple past

Note: Practice Pages utilize the generative rules introduced in the introduction to students section to encourage students to make as creative sentences as possible.

Simple Sentence
S → NP VP

Verb Phrase:
VP → (Adv) V (NP) (NP) (PP) (Adv)
VP → (Adv) V (VP) (PP) (Adv)

Noun Phrase:
NP → (Art) (Adj*) N (RC) (PP)

Adv = Adverb: *always, often, quickly, suddenly*
PP = Prepositional Phrase: *in, on, from*
Art = Article: *a, an, the*
Adj = Adjectives: *cute, fluffy, white*
RC = Relative Clause: the cat *that I saw at the shelter*

Parentheses () means optional
Asterick * means can have multiple

Past Progressive Tense

PRACTICE SENTENCES

1. _____
_____
2. _____
_____
3. _____
_____

1. _____
_____
2. _____
_____
3. _____
_____

1. _____
_____
2. _____
_____
3. _____
_____

Notes: Use this space to note common mistakes, instances you can use the tense or anything that helps you use the tense.

Past Progressive Tense

QUESTIONS IN PAST PROGRESSIVE TENSE

LEVEL I

(Where)   was   the pretty bird   singing   at 1:00pm?
(_____) _____ _____ _____ at _____ ?
   Wh-Word   Was/Were   NP   V+ing   Time

LEVEL II

(Where)   was   the worm   hiding   while   the pretty bird   was   singing?
(_____) _____ _____ _____ while _____ _____ _____ ?
   Wh-word   was/were   NP   V+ing   NP   was/were   V+ing

LEVEL III

(Where)   was   the pretty bird   singing   when   the branch   suddenly   broke?
(_____) _____ _____ _____ when _____ suddenly _____ ?
   Wh-word   was/were   NP   V+ing   NP   V+simple past

Note: Practice Pages utilize the generative rules introduced in the introduction to students section to encourage students to make as creative sentences as possible.

Simple Sentence
S → NP VP

Verb Phrase:
VP → (Adv) V (NP) (NP) (PP) (Adv)
VP → (Adv) V (VP) (PP) (Adv)

Noun Phrase:
NP → (Art) (Adj*) N (RC) (PP)

Adv = Adverb: *always, often, quickly, suddenly*
PP = Prepositional Phrase: *in, on, from*
Art = Article: *a, an, the*
Adj = Adjectives: *cute, fluffy, white*
RC = Relative Clause: the cat *that I saw at the shelter*

Parentheses () means optional
Asterick * means can have multiple

Past Progressive Tense

PRACTICE SENTENCES

1. _____
   _____
2. _____
   _____
3. _____
   _____

1. _____
   _____
2. _____
   _____
3. _____
   _____

1. _____
   _____
2. _____
   _____
3. _____
   _____

Notes: Use this space to note common mistakes, instances you can use the tense or anything that helps you use the tense.

Past Progressive Tense

NEGATIVE STATEMENTS IN PAST PROGRESSIVE TENSE

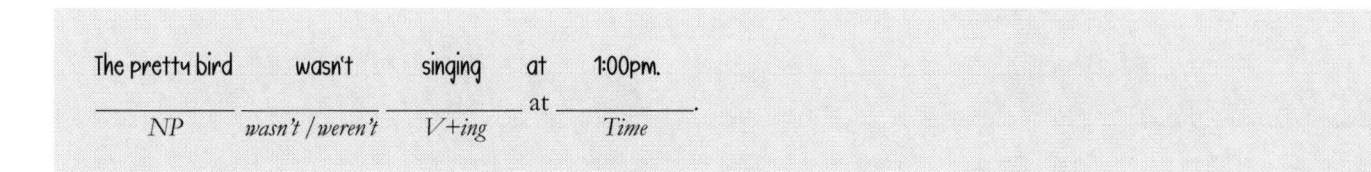

LEVEL I

The pretty bird   wasn't   singing   at   1:00pm.
_____ _____ _____ at _____.
      NP   wasn't / weren't   V+ing   Time

LEVEL II

The pretty bird   wasn't   singing   while   the worm   was   hiding.
_____ _____ _____ while _____ _____ _____.
      NP   wasn't / weren't   V+ing   NP   was/were   V+ing

LEVEL III

The pretty bird   wasn't   singing   when suddenly   the worm   appeared.
_____ _____ _____ when suddenly _____ _____.
      NP   wasn't / weren't   V+ing   NP   V+simple past

Note: Practice Pages utilize the generative rules introduced in the introduction to students section to encourage students to make as creative sentences as possible.

Simple Sentence
S → NP VP

Verb Phrase:
VP → (Adv) V (NP) (NP) (PP) (Adv)
VP → (Adv) V (VP) (PP) (Adv)

Noun Phrase:
NP → (Art) (Adj*) N (RC) (PP)

Adv = Adverb: *always, often, quickly, suddenly*
PP = Prepositional Phrase: *in, on, from*
Art = Article: *a, an, the*
Adj = Adjectives: *cute, fluffy, white*
RC = Relative Clause: the cat *that I saw at the shelter*

Parentheses () means optional
Asterick * means can have multiple

Past Progressive Tense

PRACTICE SENTENCES

1. _____
   _____
2. _____
   _____
3. _____
   _____

1. _____
   _____
2. _____
   _____
3. _____
   _____

1. _____
   _____
2. _____
   _____
3. _____
   _____

Notes: Use this space to note common mistakes, instances you can use the tense or anything that helps you use the tense.

Past Progressive Tense

MODAL STATEMENTS IN PAST PROGRESSIVE TENSE

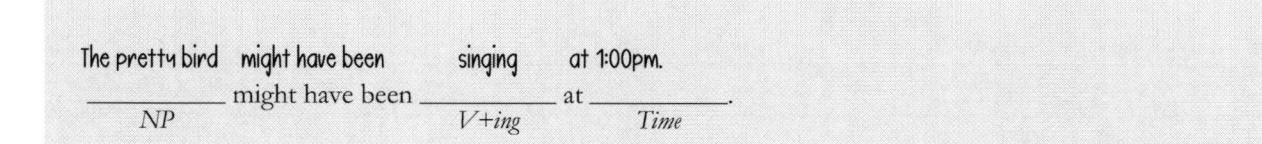

LEVEL I

The pretty bird might have been singing at 1:00pm.
_____ might have been _____ at _____.
  NP   V+ing   Time

LEVEL II

The pretty bird might have been singing while the worm was hiding.
_____ might have been _____ while _____ _____ _____.
  NP   V+ing   NP   was/were   V+ing

LEVEL III

The pretty bird might have been singing when the slender branch suddenly broke.
_____ might have been _____ when _____ suddenly _____.
  NP   V+ing   NP   V+simple past

Note: Practice Pages utilize the generative rules introduced in the introduction to students section to encourage students to make as creative sentences as possible.

Simple Sentence
S → NP VP

Verb Phrase:
VP → (Adv) V (NP) (NP) (PP) (Adv)
VP → (Adv) V (VP) (PP) (Adv)

Noun Phrase:
NP → (Art) (Adj*) N (RC) (PP)

Adv = Adverb: *always, often, quickly, suddenly*
PP = Prepositional Phrase: *in, on, from*
Art = Article: *a, an, the*
Adj = Adjectives: *cute, fluffy, white*
RC = Relative Clause: the cat *that I saw at the shelter*

Parentheses () means optional
Asterick * means can have multiple

Past Progressive Tense

PRACTICE SENTENCES

1. _____
   _____
2. _____
   _____
3. _____
   _____

1. _____
   _____
2. _____
   _____
3. _____
   _____

1. _____
   _____
2. _____
   _____
3. _____
   _____

Notes: Use this space to note common mistakes, instances you can use the tense or anything that helps you use the tense.

Past Progressive Tense

NOUN CLAUSES STATEMENTS IN PAST PROGRESSIVE TENSE

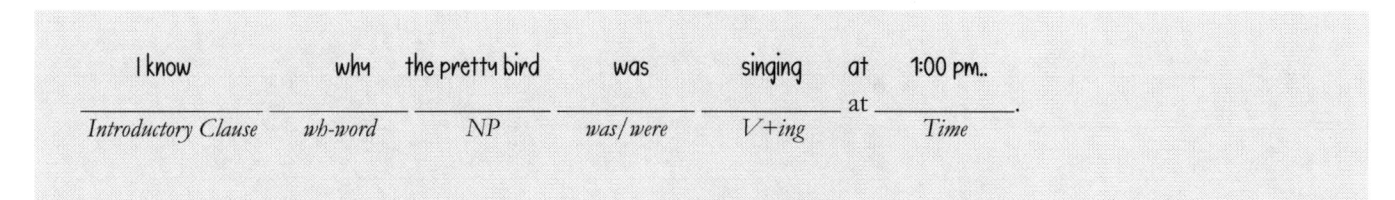

LEVEL I

I know	why	the pretty bird	was	singing	at	1:00 pm.
Introductory Clause	wh-word	NP	was/were	V+ing	at	Time

LEVEL II

I know	why	the worm	was	hiding	while	the pretty bird	was	singing.
Introductory Clause	wh-word	NP	was/were	V+ing	while	NP	was/were	V+ing

LEVEL III

I know	why	the pretty bird	was	singing	when	the slender branch	broke	suddenly.
Introductory Clause	wh-word	NP	was/were	V+ing	when	NP	V+simple past	suddenly.

Note: Practice Pages utilize the generative rules introduced in the introduction to students section to encourage students to make as creative sentences as possible.

Simple Sentence
S → NP VP

Verb Phrase:
VP → (Adv) V (NP) (NP) (PP) (Adv)
VP → (Adv) V (VP) (PP) (Adv)

Noun Phrase:
NP → (Art) (Adj*) N (RC) (PP)

Adv = Adverb: *always, often, quickly, suddenly*
PP = Prepositional Phrase: *in, on, from*
Art = Article: *a, an, the*
Adj = Adjectives: *cute, fluffy, white*
RC = Relative Clause: the cat *that I saw at the shelter*

Parentheses () means optional
Asterick * means can have multiple

Past Progressive Tense

PRACTICE SENTENCES

1. _____
_____
2. _____
_____
3. _____
_____

1. _____
_____
2. _____
_____
3. _____
_____

1. _____
_____
2. _____
_____
3. _____
_____

Notes: Use this space to note common mistakes, instances you can use the tense or anything that helps you use the tense.

PRESENT PERFECT TENSE

Rules

The present perfect is used for:

* Experiences at an unspecified past time (often with already or never)
I <u>have already read</u> that book.

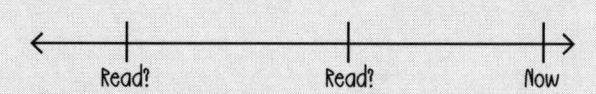

<--|--------|--------|-->
   Read?   Read?   Now

* Multiple recent actions
We have watched that movie five times this year.

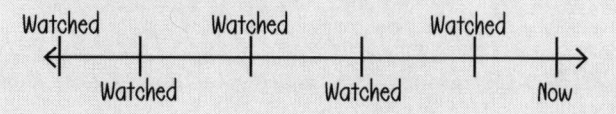

    Watched   Watched   Watched
<--|----|----|----|----|-->
     Watched   Watched   Now

* Situations that began in the past and have continued until now.
I <u>have known</u> her for thirty years.

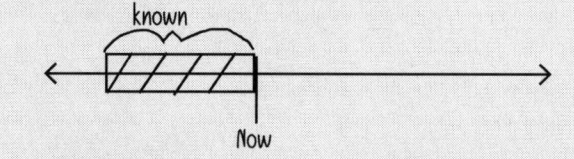

known
<--[////]-------->
      Now

* Gradual change over time
She <u>has changed</u> a lot over the past year.

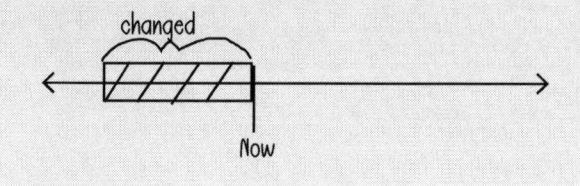

changed
<--[////]-------->
      Now

I.I Warm Up

What things are the same now as when you were a child?

Ever since I was a child...

1. I have loved music.

2.

3.

4.

5.

Present Perfect Tense Forms

I	have	already	worked.
He She It	has		worked.
You We They	have		worked.

Negative Present Perfect Tense Forms

I	haven't	worked	yet.
He She It	hasn't	worked	
You We They	haven't	worked	

Yes-No Qs Present Pefect Tense Forms

Have	I	worked	already?
Has	he she it	worked	
Have	you we they	worked	

Wh Qs Present Perfect Tense Forms

Where	have	I	worked	so far?
Why	has	he she it	worked	
Where	have	you we they	worked	

Present Perfect Tense

Level I sentences

One clause. Duration with always

1. The cat <u>has</u> always <u>loved</u> milk.

The _____ _____ _____ .
     noun   *has always verbed*   *object*

Level II sentences

One clause. Duration with for and since.

2. The cat has loved milk <u>for many years.</u>

The _____ _____ _____ for _____ .
    noun   *has verbed*   *object*   *length of time*

3. The cat has loved milk <u>since January</u>.

The _____ _____ _____ since _____ .
    noun   *has verbed*   *object*   *start time*

Level III sentences

Since + second clause in simple past.

4. The cat has loved milk <u>ever</u> <u>since she was a kitten</u>.

The _____ _____ _____ ever since
    noun   *has verbed*   *object*

_____ _____ .
    noun/ pronoun   *was/ were + compliment*

5. The cat has loved milk <u>ever since she first tasted it.</u>

The _____ _____ _____ ever since
    noun   *has verbed*   *object*

_____ _____ .
    noun/ pronoun   *verbed + object*

Level IV sentences

Two clauses in present perfect with "for as long as."

6. The cat has loved milk <u>for as long as she has lived in the barn</u>.

The _____ _____ _____ for as long as
    noun   *has verbed*   *object*

_____ _____ _____ .
 noun/pronoun   *has verbed*   *object*

Present Perfect Tense

LET'S ASK SOME QUESTIONS

Take a couple of your sentences. Write four questions. Use "ever" or "how long" + for (optional).

Example:

Have you ever seen Paris?   How long have you lived here for?

Has	noun/ nouns	ever verbed	object

How long has	noun/ nouns	verbed + object	(for)

1. _____?
2. _____?
3. _____?
4. _____?

> Since the present perfect commonly talks about duration and experience "have + ever" and "how long has" are commonly used.
>
> Examples:
>
> *Have you ever eaten kapsa?*
>
> *How long have they known each other for?*
>
> *Has she ever been to the city?*
>
> *How long has he studied English?*

NOW ANSWER WITH A NOUN CLAUSE

Pick one of the introductory clauses below:

It doesn't matter   I don't know   It's not important   It's not clear   I can't say

I don't care <u>whether or not</u> you have ever seen Paris.
          (if)
It doesn't matter <u>how long</u> you have lived her.

Introductory clause	whether or not/ if	noun(s)	have ever verbed + obj

Introductory clause	how long	noun(s)	have verbed + obj +for

Write four answers to the questions above using an introductory clause.

1. _____
2. _____
3. _____
4. _____

> Questions of the form, "Has she ever seen Paris?" are yes/no questions. When yes/no questions become noun-clauses they take *if* or *whether or not.*
>
> Examples:
>
> *I don't know if she has ever gone fishing.*

Present Perfect Tense

CONDITIONS AND CONSEQUENCES

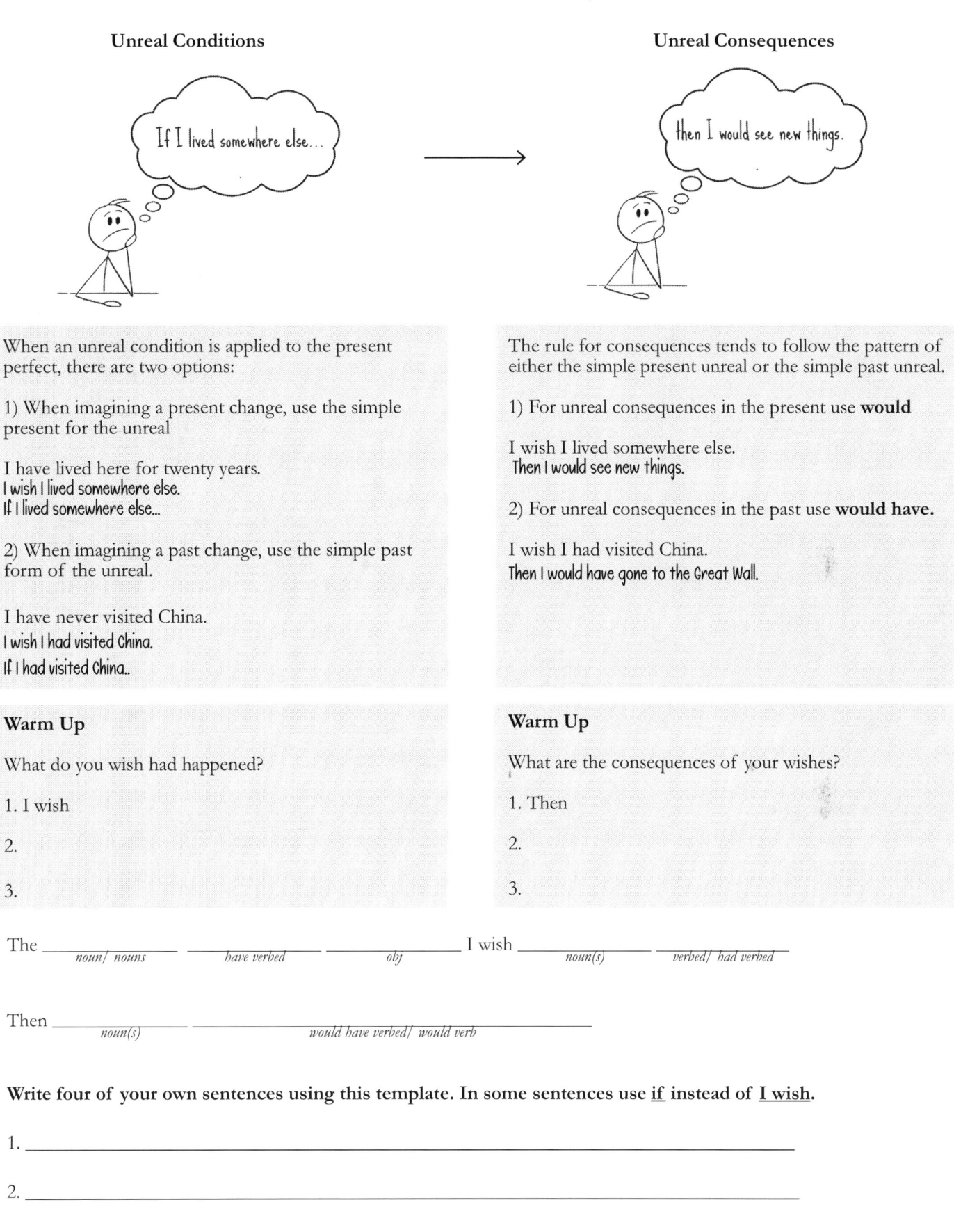

Unreal Conditions

(If I lived somewhere else...)

Unreal Consequences

(then I would see new things.)

When an unreal condition is applied to the present perfect, there are two options:

1) When imagining a present change, use the simple present for the unreal

I have lived here for twenty years.
I wish I lived somewhere else.
If I lived somewhere else...

2) When imagining a past change, use the simple past form of the unreal.

I have never visited China.
I wish I had visited China.
If I had visited China..

The rule for consequences tends to follow the pattern of either the simple present unreal or the simple past unreal.

1) For unreal consequences in the present use **would**

I wish I lived somewhere else.
Then I would see new things.

2) For unreal consequences in the past use **would have**.

I wish I had visited China.
Then I would have gone to the Great Wall.

Warm Up

What do you wish had happened?

1. I wish

2.

3.

Warm Up

What are the consequences of your wishes?

1. Then

2.

3.

The _____ _____ _____ I wish _____ _____
　　　noun/ nouns　　*have verbed*　　*obj*　　　　　　*noun(s)*　　*verbed/ had verbed*

Then _____ _____
　　　noun(s)　　*would have verbed/ would verb*

Write four of your own sentences using this template. In some sentences use <u>if</u> instead of <u>I wish</u>.

1. _____

2. _____

3. _____

4 _____

Present Perfect Tense

PRACTICAL APPLICATION

Read the following short paragraph. <u>Underline</u> present perfect verbs. (Circle) the conditionals.

Old Town/New Town

I have lived in this town for twenty years, and, in that time, I have witnessed quite a few changes. When I first moved here, it was little one-horse nowhere. There was a post office, a restaurant, and a church. That's it. Now everything has started to sprawl in all directions. The farm fields have been reshaped by new developments. They've built towering complexes near the main drag. Shopping centers, and office buildings have sprung up. The skyline has grown. The once sleepy streets have become centers of hustle and bustle. The population has spiked exponentially. The old-timers say, "Look at all these swarms of people! Look at these mobs!" They've built a bowling alley, an ice-skating rink, and even a nightclub. These changes have made things more exciting, though they've also driven up prices a bit. The price of a house has more than tripled! I don't know why the floodgates have been opened. Maybe someone has struck oil. Or maybe everyone has just come to see me! I mostly like the way things are now. But I would change one thing. There's so much light pollution at night. I wish I could still go outside and see the stars.

NOTES: Use this space to write notes on the usage of the tense.

---

witness: see

one-horse nowhere: very small town

sprawl: stretch

tower: rise high

main drag: main road

spring up: grow fast

skyline: city roofs

hustle and buslte: lots of activity and movement

spike: rapid increase

old timers: old residents of a place

swarms: masses

mobs: swarms of people

drive up: increase

open the floodgates: cause a rapid increase in something

light pollution: excessive light

Now you try! Write a paragraph in which you describe how something has changed over time.

Present Perfect Tense

SENTENCES IN PRESENT PERFECT

LEVEL I

The cat / has / always / loved milk.

___NP___ ___has/have___ always ___VP+past participle___ .

LEVEL II

The cat / has / loved milk / for many years.

___NP___ ___has/have___ ___VP+past participle___ for ___time___ .

LEVEL III

The cat / has / loved milk / ever since / she was a kitten.

___NP___ ___hasn't/haven't___ ___VP+past participle___ ever since ___clause___ .

Note: Practice Pages utilize the generative rules introduced in the introduction to students section to encourage students to make as creative sentences as possible.

Simple Sentence
S → NP VP

Verb Phrase:
VP → (Adv) V (NP) (NP) (PP) (Adv)
VP → (Adv) V (VP) (PP) (Adv)

Noun Phrase:
NP → (Art) (Adj*) N (RC) (PP)

Adv = Adverb: *always, often, quickly, suddenly*
PP = Prepositional Phrase: *in, on, from*
Art = Article: *a, an, the*
Adj = Adjectives: *cute, fluffy, white*
RC = Relative Clause: the cat *that I saw at the shelter*

Parentheses () means optional
Asterick * means can have multiple

Present Perfect Tense

PRACTICE SENTENCES

1. _____
2. _____
3. _____

1. _____
2. _____
3. _____

1. _____
2. _____
3. _____

Notes: Use this space to note common mistakes, instances you can use the tense or anything that helps you use the tense.

Present Perfect Tense

QUESTIONS IN PRESENT PERFECT TENSE

LEVEL I

(Why) has the cat always loved milk?

(_____) _____ _____ always _____ ?
Wh-word | has/have | NP | VP+Past Participle

LEVEL II

(Why) has the cat loved milk for many years?

(_____) _____ _____ _____ for _____ ?
Why | Has/Have | NP | VP+Past Participle | time

LEVEL III

(Why) has the cat loved milk ever since she was a kitten?

(_____) _____ _____ _____ ever since _____ ?
Wh-word | has/have | NP | VP+Past Participle | clause

Note: Practice Pages utilize the generative rules introduced in the introduction to students section to encourage students to make as creative sentences as possible.

Simple Sentence
S → NP VP

Verb Phrase:
VP → (Adv) V (NP) (NP) (PP) (Adv)
VP → (Adv) V (VP) (PP) (Adv)

Noun Phrase:
NP → (Art) (Adj*) N (RC) (PP)

Adv = Adverb: *always, often, quickly, suddenly*
PP = Prepositional Phrase: *in, on, from*
Art = Article: *a, an, the*
Adj = Adjectives: *cute, fluffy, white*
RC = Relative Clause: the cat *that I saw at the shelter*

Parentheses () means optional
Asterick * means can have multiple

Present Perfect Tense

PRACTICE SENTENCES

1. _____
_____
2. _____
_____
3. _____
_____

1. _____
_____
2. _____
_____
3. _____
_____

1. _____
_____
2. _____
_____
3. _____
_____

Notes: Use this space to note common mistakes, instances you can use the tense or anything that helps you use the tense.

Present Perfect Tense

NEGATIVE STATEMENTS IN PRESENT PERFECT TENSE

LEVEL I

The cat   hasn't   always   loved milk.
_____ _____ always _____ .
   NP   hasn't / haven't   VP+past participle

LEVEL II

The cat   hasn't   loved milk   for many years.
_____ _____ _____ for _____ .
   NP   hasn't / haven't VP+past participle   time

LEVEL III

The cat   hasn't   loved milk   ever since   she was a kitten.
_____ _____ _____ ever since _____ .
   NP   hasn't / haven't VP+past participle   clause

Note: Practice Pages utilize the generative rules introduced in the introduction to students section to encourage students to make as creative sentences as possible.

Simple Sentence
S → NP VP

Verb Phrase:
VP → (Adv) V (NP) (NP) (PP) (Adv)
VP → (Adv) V (VP) (PP) (Adv)

Noun Phrase:
NP → (Art) (Adj*) N (RC) (PP)

Adv = Adverb: *always, often, quickly, suddenly*
PP = Prepositional Phrase: *in, on, from*
Art = Article: *a, an, the*
Adj = Adjectives: *cute, fluffy, white*
RC = Relative Clause: the cat *that I saw at the shelter*

Parentheses () means optional
Asterick * means can have multiple

Present Perfect Tense

PRACTICE SENTENCES

1. _____
   _____
2. _____
   _____
3. _____
   _____

1. _____
   _____
2. _____
   _____
3. _____
   _____

1. _____
   _____
2. _____
   _____
3. _____
   _____

Notes: Use this space to note common mistakes, instances you can use the tense or anything that helps you use the tense.

Present Perfect Tense

MODAL STATEMENTS IN PRESENT PERFECT TENSE

LEVEL I

The cat   might have   drunk all the milk.

_____ might have _____.
   NP   *VP+past participle*

LEVEL II

The cat   might have   drunk milk   for   many years.

_____ might have _____ for _____.
   NP   *VP+past participle*   *time*

LEVEL III

The cat   might have   drunk milk   ever since   she was a kitten.

_____ might have _____ ever since _____.
   NP   *VP+past participle*   *clause*

Note: Practice Pages utilize the generative rules introduced in the introduction to students section to encourage students to make as creative sentences as possible.

Simple Sentence
S → NP VP

Verb Phrase:
VP → (Adv) V (NP) (NP) (PP) (Adv)
VP → (Adv) V (VP) (PP) (Adv)

Noun Phrase:
NP → (Art) (Adj*) N (RC) (PP)

Adv = Adverb: *always, often, quickly, suddenly*
PP = Prepositional Phrase: *in, on, from*
Art = Article: *a, an, the*
Adj = Adjectives: *cute, fluffy, white*
RC = Relative Clause: the cat *that I saw at the shelter*

Parentheses () means optional
Asterick * means can have multiple

Present Perfect Tense

PRACTICE SENTENCES

1. _____
   _____
2. _____
   _____
3. _____
   _____

1. _____
   _____
2. _____
   _____
3. _____
   _____

1. _____
   _____
2. _____
   _____
3. _____
   _____

Notes: Use this space to note common mistakes, instances you can use the tense or anything that helps you use the tense.

Present Perfect Tense

NOUN CLAUSES STATEMENTS IN PRESENT PERFECT TENSE

LEVEL I

I know	why	the cat	has	always loved milk.
Introductory Clause	wh-word	NP	has/have	VP past participle

LEVEL II

I know	why	the cat	has	loved milk	for	many years.
Introductory Clause	wh-word	NP	has/have	VP past participle	for	time

LEVEL III

I know	why	the cat	has	loved milk	ever since	she was a kitten.
Introductory Clause	wh-word	NP	has/have	VP past participle	ever since	clause

Note: Practice Pages utilize the generative rules introduced in the introduction to students section to encourage students to make as creative sentences as possible.

Simple Sentence
S → NP VP

Verb Phrase:
VP → (Adv) V (NP) (NP) (PP) (Adv)
VP → (Adv) V (VP) (PP) (Adv)

Noun Phrase:
NP → (Art) (Adj*) N (RC) (PP)

Adv = Adverb: *always, often, quickly, suddenly*
PP = Prepositional Phrase: *in, on, from*
Art = Article: *a, an, the*
Adj = Adjectives: *cute, fluffy, white*
RC = Relative Clause: the cat *that I saw at the shelter*

Parentheses () means optional
Asterick * means can have multiple

94

Present Perfect Tense

PRACTICE SENTENCES

1. _____
   _____
2. _____
   _____
3. _____
   _____

1. _____
   _____
2. _____
   _____
3. _____
   _____

1. _____
   _____
2. _____
   _____
3. _____
   _____

Notes: Use this space to note common mistakes, instances you can use the tense or anything that helps you use the tense.

PRESENT PERFECT PROGRESSIVE TENSE

Rules

The present perfect progressive is used for:

* Actions which began in the past and are still in progress (with since and for)
I have been walking for days.
I have been walking since Monday.

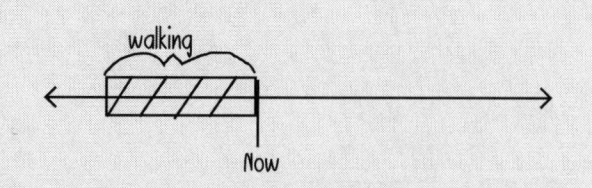

* Recent actions which are still in progress (with "just" or "lately")
I've been watching a lot of movies lately.
I've just been reading

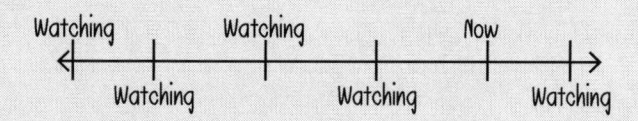

I.I Warm Up

How long have you been doing all the things you are doing right now?

1. I have been studying for five years.

2.

3.

4.

5.

Simple Present Perfect Progressive Forms

I	have been	working	for days.
He She It	has been	working	
You We They	have been	working	

Negative Present Perfect Progressive Forms

I	haven't been	working	for days.
He She It	hasn't been	working	
You We They	haven't been	working	

Yes-No Qs Present Perfect Progressive Forms

Have	I	been working	for days?
Has	he she it	been working	
Have	you we they	been working	

Wh Qs Present Perfect Progressive Forms

How long	have	I	been working?	
Why	has	he she it	been working	all night?
Where	have	you we they	been working	this year?

Level I sentences

One clause. Duration.

1. The fish <u>has been swimming</u> a lot lately.

The _____ _____ _____ a lot lately.
       noun   *has been verbing*   *object*

2. The fish <u>has been swimming</u> for hours.

The _____ _____ _____ for _____.
       noun   *has been verbing*   *object*   *length of time*

Level II sentences

One clause. Duration with for and since.

3. The fish has been swimming since this morning.

The _____ _____ _____ since _____.
       noun   *has been verbing*   *object*   *start time*

Level III sentences

Since + second clause in simple past.

4. The fish has been swimming <u>ever</u> <u>since she was in the water</u>.

The _____ _____ _____ ever since
       noun   *has been verbing*   *object*

_____ _____.
       noun/ pronoun   *was/ were + compliment*

5. The fish has been swimming <u>ever since she first opened her eyes</u>.

The _____ _____ _____ ever since
       noun   *has been verbing*   *object*

_____ _____.
       noun/ pronoun   *verbed + object*

6. The fish has been swimming <u>for as long as the sea has been breaking</u>.

Level IV sentences

Two clauses in present perfect with "for as long as."

The _____ _____ _____ for as long as
       noun   *has been verbing*   *object*

_____ _____ _____.
  noun/pronoun   *has been verbing*   *object*

Present Perfect Progressive Tense

LET'S ASK SOME QUESTIONS

Take a couple of your sentences. Write four questions. "How long" + for (optional) or "where"

Example:

How long have you been playing violin (for)? Where have you been living?

_____ _____ _____ _____
How long has/have   noun/ nouns been verbing (for) compliment

_____ _____ _____ _____
Where has/have   noun/ nouns been verbing   compliment

1. _____

2. _____

3. _____

4. _____

> Since the present perfect commonly talks about duration of actions. "How long" and "where" are the most common question forms.
>
> Examples:
>
> *How long have they been working at Amazon?*
>
> *Where has she been studying?*
>
> *How long have the friends been talking on the phone?*
>
> *Where have they been going to the gym?*

NOW ANSWER WITH A NOUN CLAUSE

Pick one of the introductory clauses below:
It doesn't matter   I don't know   It's not important   It's not clear   I can't say

I don't care <u>whether or not</u> you have ever seen Paris.
              (if)
It doesn't matter <u>how long</u> you have lived her.

_____ _____ _____ _____
Introductory clause how long   noun(s)   have been verbing

_____ _____ _____ _____
Introductory clause   where   noun(s)   have been verbing

Write four answers to the questions above using an introductory clause.

1. _____

2. _____

3. _____

4. _____

> The present perfect progressive uses the regular subject verb object order following noun clauses.
>
> Examples:
>
> *I don't know how long she has been studying.*
>
> *It doesn't matter where they have been living.*
>
> *I can't say where they've been going.*
>
> *It's not clear how long he's been practicing Chinese.*

Present Perfect Progressive Tense

CONDITIONS AND CONSEQUENCES

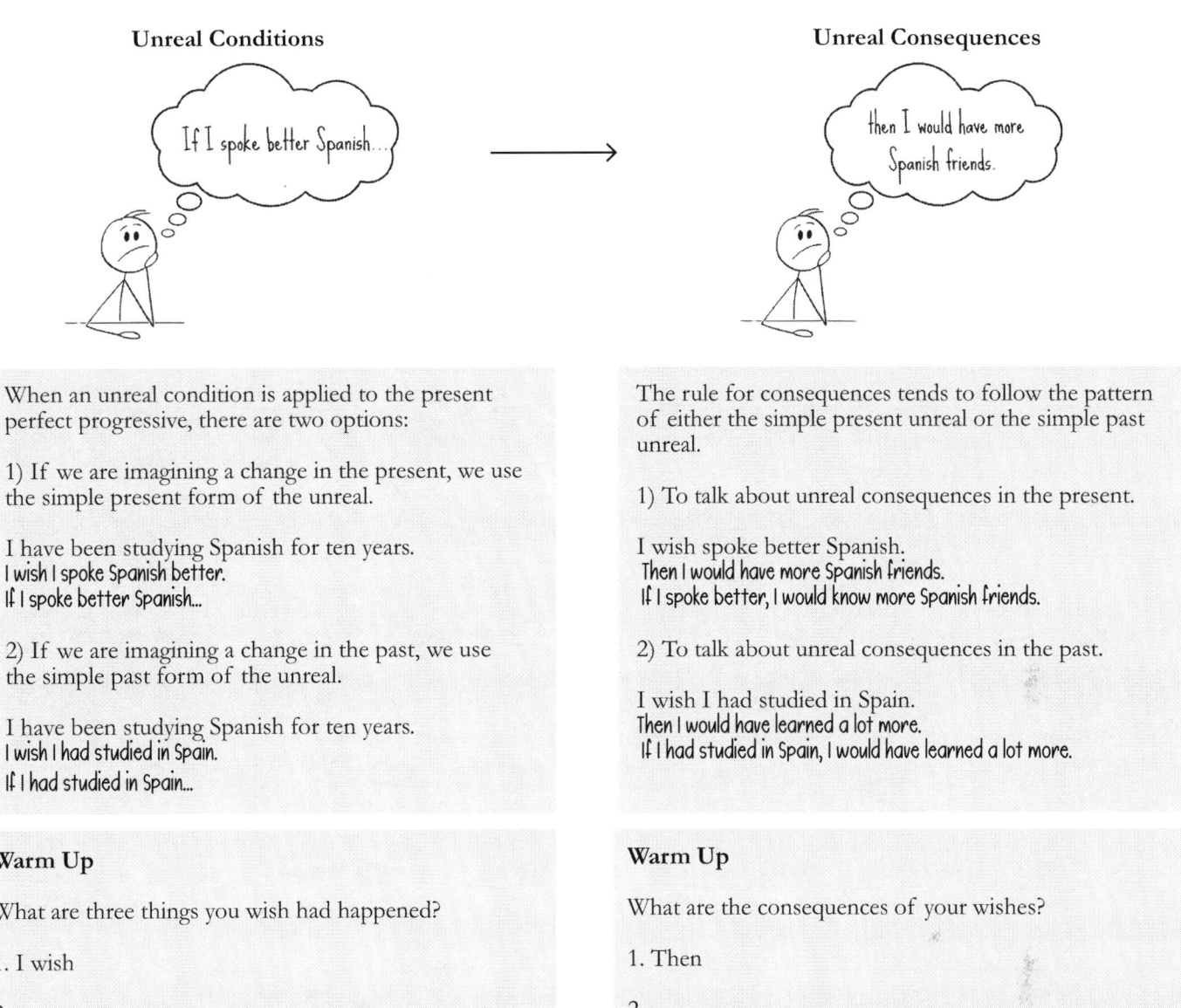

Unreal Conditions

If I spoke better Spanish...

→

Unreal Consequences

then I would have more Spanish friends.

When an unreal condition is applied to the present perfect progressive, there are two options:

1) If we are imagining a change in the present, we use the simple present form of the unreal.

I have been studying Spanish for ten years.
I wish I spoke Spanish better.
If I spoke better Spanish...

2) If we are imagining a change in the past, we use the simple past form of the unreal.

I have been studying Spanish for ten years.
I wish I had studied in Spain.
If I had studied in Spain...

The rule for consequences tends to follow the pattern of either the simple present unreal or the simple past unreal.

1) To talk about unreal consequences in the present.

I wish spoke better Spanish.
Then I would have more Spanish friends.
If I spoke better, I would know more Spanish friends.

2) To talk about unreal consequences in the past.

I wish I had studied in Spain.
Then I would have learned a lot more.
If I had studied in Spain, I would have learned a lot more.

Warm Up

What are three things you wish had happened?

1. I wish

2.

3.

Warm Up

What are the consequences of your wishes?

1. Then

2.

3.

The _____ _____ _____ I wish _____ _____
     noun/ nouns   *have been verbing*   *obj*   *noun(s)*   *verbed/ had verbed*

Then _____ _____
      noun(s)   *would have verbed/ would verb*

Write four of your own sentences using this template. In some sentences use *if* instead of *I wish*.

1. _____

2. _____

3. _____

4. _____

Present Perfect Progressive Tense

PRACTICAL APPLICATION

Read the following short paragraph. Underline the verbs in present perfect continous. Circle the conditionals.

New Hobbies

Ever since I first came to America, I've really been **living it up**. At home, I worked a ton of hours. But now I have a lot more free time, so I've been **indulging in** all sorts of hobbies and interests. For example, I recently signed up for an art class. We've been studying **watercolors** for two weeks now. I just painted a great apple. Next week, I'll draw a chair. I've been **getting a lot out of** the course, and I've been finding that exploring my creativity is a very satisfying way to spend my time. I've also been developing something of a **green thumb**. I have a community garden in my apartment and I've been planting all sorts of flowers, fruits, and vegetables. My favorite is my sunflower. When I first planted it, it was just a tiny, little **sprig**. But now it has a big yellow flower **packed with** seeds. It's been growing and growing. Finally, I've been making a lot of new friends. I joined a birdwatching club last week. We've been going out with our binoculars every morning and learning about new birds. Yesterday, I saw a big, blue **heron**. All in all I've been having a great time. I wish I had come earlier. Then I would have had even more time for painting, gardening, and birdwatching.

NOTES: Use this space to write notes about the usage of the tense.

---

living it up: enjoying life

indulging in: partaking of a special treat

watercolors: type of painting

getting a lot out of: learning a lot

green thumb: talent for gardening

sprig: tiny plant

packed with: full of

heron: big hunting bird

Now you try! Write a paragraph in which you describe the new things you have been doing since you came to the United States.

Present Perfect Progressive Tense

SENTENCES IN PRESENT PERFECT PROGRESSIVE TENSE

LEVEL I

The fish has been swimming lately.
_____ _____ been _____ _____ .
    NP   has/have   Ving   adverb

LEVEL II

The fish has been swimming for hours.
_____ _____ been _____ for _____ .
    NP   have/has   Ving   duration

LEVEL III

The fish has been swimming ever since she was put in the fish bowl.
_____ _____ been _____ ever since _____ .
    NP   have/has   Ving   clause

Note: Practice Pages utilize the generative rules introduced in the introduction to students section to encourage students to make as creative sentences as possible.

Simple Sentence
S → NP VP

Verb Phrase:
VP → (Adv) V (NP) (NP) (PP) (Adv)
VP → (Adv) V (VP) (PP) (Adv)

Noun Phrase:
NP → (Art) (Adj*) N (RC) (PP)

Adv = Adverb: *always, often, quickly, suddenly*
PP = Prepositional Phrase: *in, on, from*
Art = Article: *a, an, the*
Adj = Adjectives: *cute, fluffy, white*
RC = Relative Clause: the cat *that I saw at the shelter*

Parentheses () means optional
Asterick * means can have multiple

Present Perfect Progressive Tense

PRACTICE SENTENCES

1. _____
   _____
2. _____
   _____
3. _____
   _____

1. _____
   _____
2. _____
   _____
3. _____
   _____

1. _____
   _____
2. _____
   _____
3. _____
   _____

Notes: Use this space to note common mistakes, instances you can use the tense or anything that helps you use the tense.

Present Perfect Progressive Tense

QUESTIONS IN PRESENT PERFECT PROGRESSIVE TENSE

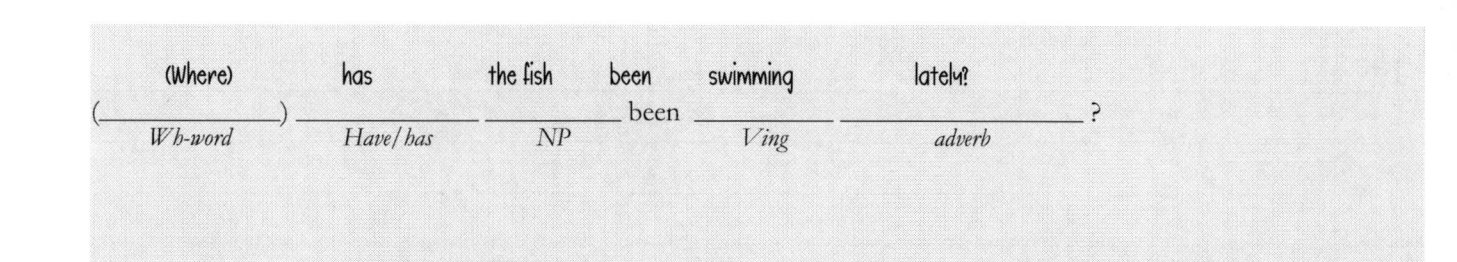

LEVEL I

(<u>(Where)</u>) <u>has</u> <u>the fish</u> been <u>swimming</u> <u>lately?</u> ?
(__Wh-word__) __Have/has__ __NP__ been __Ving__ __adverb__

LEVEL II

(<u>(Where)</u>) <u>has</u> <u>the fish</u> been <u>swimming</u> for <u>hours?</u> ?
(__Wh-word__) __Have/has__ __NP__ been __Ving__ for __duration__

LEVEL III

<u>Why</u> <u>has</u> <u>the fish</u> been <u>swimming</u> ever since <u>she was put in the fish bowl?</u> ?
__Wh-word__ __Have/has__ __NP__ been __Ving__ ever since __clause__

Note: Practice Pages utilize the generative rules introduced in the introduction to students section to encourage students to make as creative sentences as possible.

Simple Sentence
S → NP VP

Verb Phrase:
VP → (Adv) V (NP) (NP) (PP) (Adv)
VP → (Adv) V (VP) (PP) (Adv)

Noun Phrase:
NP → (Art) (Adj*) N (RC) (PP)

Adv = Adverb: *always, often, quickly, suddenly*
PP = Prepositional Phrase: *in, on, from*
Art = Article: *a, an, the*
Adj = Adjectives: *cute, fluffy, white*
RC = Relative Clause: the cat *that I saw at the shelter*

Parentheses () means optional
Asterick * means can have multiple

Present Perfect Progressive Tense

PRACTICE SENTENCES

1. _____
_____
2. _____
_____
3. _____
_____

1. _____
_____
2. _____
_____
3. _____
_____

1. _____
_____
2. _____
_____
3. _____
_____

Notes: Use this space to note common mistakes, instances you can use the tense or anything that helps you use the tense.

Present Perfect Progressive Tense

NEGATIVE STATEMENTS IN PRESENT PERFECT PROGRESSIVE TENSE

LEVEL I

The fish hasn't been swimming lately.
_____ _____ been _____ _____.
   NP   hasn't/haven't   Ving   adverb

LEVEL II

The fish hasn't been swimming for hours.
_____ _____ been _____ for _____.
   NP   haven't/hasn't   Ving   duration

LEVEL III

The fish hasn't been swimming ever since she was put in the fish bowl.
_____ _____ been _____ ever since _____.
   NP   haven't/hasn't   Ving   clause

Note: Practice Pages utilize the generative rules introduced in the introduction to students section to encourage students to make as creative sentences as possible.

Simple Sentence
S → NP VP

Verb Phrase:
VP → (Adv) V (NP) (NP) (PP) (Adv)
VP → (Adv) V (VP) (PP) (Adv)

Noun Phrase:
NP → (Art) (Adj*) N (RC) (PP)

Adv = Adverb: *always, often, quickly, suddenly*
PP = Prepositional Phrase: *in, on, from*
Art = Article: *a, an, the*
Adj = Adjectives: *cute, fluffy, white*
RC = Relative Clause: the cat *that I saw at the shelter*

Parentheses () means optional
Asterick * means can have multiple

Present Perfect Progressive Tense

PRACTICE SENTENCES

1. _____
_____
2. _____
_____
3. _____
_____

1. _____
_____
2. _____
_____
3. _____
_____

1. _____
_____
2. _____
_____
3. _____
_____

Notes: Use this space to note common mistakes, instances you can use the tense or anything that helps you use the tense.

Present Perfect Progressive Tense

MODAL IN PRESENT PERFECT PROGRESSIVE TENSE

LEVEL I

The fish might have been swimming lately.
_____ might have been _____ _____ .
   NP   Ving   adverb

LEVEL II

The fish might have been swimming for hours.
_____ might have been _____ for _____ .
   NP   Ving   duration

LEVEL III

The fish might have been swimming ever since she was put in the fish bowl.
_____ might have been _____ ever since _____ .
   NP   Ving   duration

Note: Practice Pages utilize the generative rules introduced in the introduction to students section to encourage students to make as creative sentences as possible.

Simple Sentence
S → NP VP

Verb Phrase:
VP → (Adv) V (NP) (NP) (PP) (Adv)
VP → (Adv) V (VP) (PP) (Adv)

Noun Phrase:
NP → (Art) (Adj*) N (RC) (PP)

Adv = Adverb: *always, often, quickly, suddenly*
PP = Prepositional Phrase: *in, on, from*
Art = Article: *a, an, the*
Adj = Adjectives: *cute, fluffy, white*
RC = Relative Clause: the cat *that I saw at the shelter*

Parentheses () means optional
Asterick * means can have multiple

108

Present Perfect Progressive Tense

PRACTICE SENTENCES

1. _____
_____
2. _____
_____
3. _____
_____

1. _____
_____
2. _____
_____
3. _____
_____

1. _____
_____
2. _____
_____
3. _____
_____

Notes: Use this space to note common mistakes, instances you can use the tense or anything that helps you use the tense.

Present Perfect Progressive Tense

NOUN CLAUSES IN PRESENT PERFECT PROGRESSIVE TENSE

LEVEL I

I know	why	the fish	has	been	swimming	lately.
Introductory Clause	wh-word	NP	has/have	been	Ving	adverb

LEVEL II

I know	why	the fish	has	been	swimming	for	hours.
Introductory Clause	wh-word	NP	has/have	been	Ving	for	adverb

LEVEL III

I know	why	the fish	has	been	swimming	ever since	she was put in the fish bowl.
Introductory Clause	wh-word	NP	has/have	been	Ving	ever since	clause

Note: Practice Pages utilize the generative rules introduced in the introduction to students section to encourage students to make as creative sentences as possible.

Simple Sentence
S → NP VP

Verb Phrase:
VP → (Adv) V (NP) (NP) (PP) (Adv)
VP → (Adv) V (VP) (PP) (Adv)

Noun Phrase:
NP → (Art) (Adj*) N (RC) (PP)

Adv = Adverb: *always, often, quickly, suddenly*
PP = Prepositional Phrase: *in, on, from*
Art = Article: *a, an, the*
Adj = Adjectives: *cute, fluffy, white*
RC = Relative Clause: the cat *that I saw at the shelter*

Parentheses () means optional
Asterick * means can have multiple

Present Perfect Progressive Tense

PRACTICE SENTENCES

1. _____
   _____
2. _____
   _____
3. _____
   _____

1. _____
   _____
2. _____
   _____
3. _____
   _____

1. _____
   _____
2. _____
   _____
3. _____
   _____

Notes: Use this space to note common mistakes, instances you can use the tense or anything that helps you use the tense.

111

Past Perfect Tense

Rules

The past perfect is used for:

* Actions which happened before another action in the past (often with "just" or "already")
At 6:00, I had just woken up.
By the time that I left, I had already eaten lunch.
I looked out the window. The grass was white. It had snowed earlier.

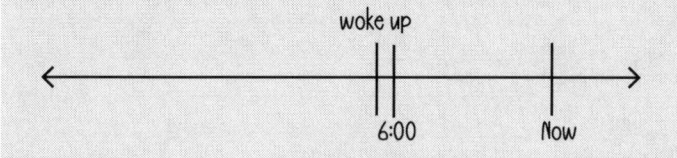

```
         woke up
<----------||----------|---------->
           6:00       Now
```

* New experiences with "never" and "until"
I had never seen a giraffe until I visited the zoo.

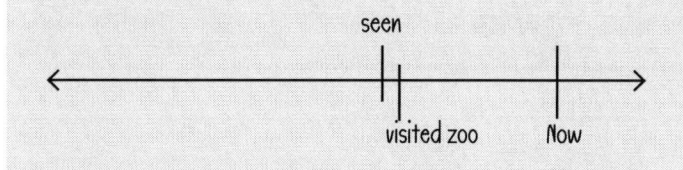

```
          seen
<----------||----------|---------->
         visited zoo  Now
```

1.1 Warm Up

Talk about the things that you had never done until you came to America.

1. I had never driven a minivan until I came here.

2.

3.

4.

5.

Simple Past Perfect Tense Forms

I	had	already	eaten.

He She It	had		eaten.

You We They	had		eaten.

Negative Past Perfect Tense Forms

I	hadn't	eaten	yet.

He She It	hadn't	eaten	

You We They	hadn't	eaten	

Yes-No Qs Past Perfect Tense Forms

Had	I	eaten	already?

Had	he she it	eaten	

	you we they	eaten	

Wh Qs Past Perfect Tense Forms

What	had	I	eaten	before vomiting?

What	had	he she it	eaten	

Where	had	you we they	eaten	

Past Perfect Tense

Level I sentences

New experiences with never + until.

Level II sentences

New experiences + never + until + second clause

Level III sentences

Simple past clause + past perfect clause + already

Level IV sentences

When clause + simple past + past perfect

1. The red fox <u>had never eaten</u> fruit until yesterday.

The _____ _____ until _____.
   adj + noun   *had never verbed + obj*   *time*

2. The red fox had never eaten fruit <u>until he climbed the apple tree</u> yesterday.

The _____ _____ until
   adj +noun   *had nver vebed + obj*

_____ _____ _____.
   noun   *verbed + obj*   *time*

3. The red fox <u>ignored</u> the fruit because he <u>had already eaten</u> breakfast.

The _____ _____ _____ because
   adj noun   *verbed*   *object*

_____ _____ _____.
   noun   *had already verbed*   *object*

4. The red fox ate the fruit <u>even though</u> he had already eaten breakfast.

The _____ _____ _____ even though
   adj noun   *verbed*   *object*

_____ _____ _____.
   noun   *had already verbed*   *object*

5. When the sun rose, the red fox licked his lips because fruit had fallen from the tree the night before.

When _____ _____ _____
        noun   *verbed*   *object*

_____ _____ _____ because
   noun   *verbed*   *object*

_____ _____ _____.
   noun   *had verbed + object*   *time word*

Past Perfect Tense

LET'S ASK SOME QUESTIONS

Asking questions in the past perfect can be a bit tricky. Since the past perfect often describes the relationship between two events, two clauses are required. These clauses are linked with "when" or "before."

Example:

Had you ever eaten kapsa before you came to Saudi Arabia?

How long had you studied English before you came to America?

___Had___ ___noun/ nouns___ ___ever verbed___ ___before noun/ nouns___ ___verbed___ ___object___

___How long had___ ___noun/ nouns___ ___verbed + object___ ___before noun/ nouns___ ___verbed___ ___object___

1. _____
2. _____
3. _____
4. _____

> Since the past perfect commonly talks about duration and experience "have + ever" and "how long had" are commonly used.
>
> Examples:
>
> *Had you ever known about Colombian history before you watched the documentary?*
>
> *How long had they known each other before they got married?*
>
> *Had she ever visited New York before she moved to the east coast?*

NOW ANSWER WITH A NOUN CLAUSE

> Pick one of the introductory clauses below:
>
> It doesn't matter   I don't know   It's not important   It's not clear   I can't say

I don't care <u>whether or not</u> she had studied English before she came to the United States.
       (if)

___Introductory clause___ ___whether or not/ if___ ___noun(s)___ ___had verbed + obj___

___before___ ___noun/ nouns___ ___verbed___ ___object___

Write four answers to the questions above using an introductory clause.

1. _____
2. _____
3. _____
4. _____

> Questions of the form, "Had she ever...." are yes/no questions. When yes/ no questions become noun-clauses they take *if* or *whether or not.*
>
> Examples:
>
> *I don't know if she had ever gone fishing before she met me.*
>
> *It doesn't matter whether or not he had gone home before he came to class.*

Past Perfect Tense

CONDITIONS AND CONSEQUENCES

Unreal Conditions

If I had gotten there earlier..

→

Unreal Consequences

Then we would have gone to see the movie

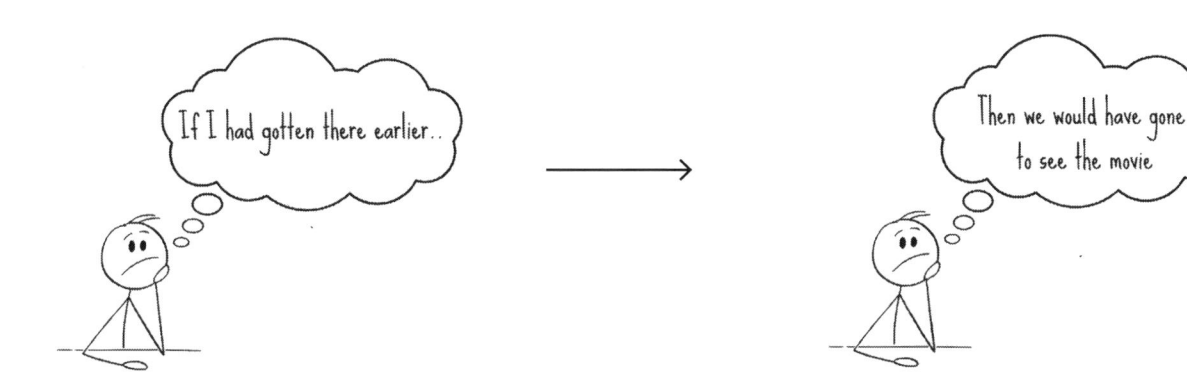

When an unreal condition is used in the past perfect, the simple past form of the conditional is used as follows: **had + past participle.**

You **had already left** by the time I came.

I wish I had gotten there earlier.
If I had gotten there earlier....

Unreal consequences in the past can often take two different forms. We can imagine consequences in the past or the present.

1) Consequences in the past.
I wish I had gotten there earlier.
Then we would have gone to see the movie

2) Consequences in the present
I fell asleep. I wish I had stayed awake.
Then I would know what happened in the movie.

Warm Up

What are three things you wish had happened?

1. I wish

2.

3.

Warm Up

What are the consequences of your wishes?

1. Then

2.

3.

The _____ _____ _____ by the time _____ _____ _____
       noun/ nouns   *had verbed*   *obj*   *noun(s)*   *verbed*   *object*

I wish _____ _____ .Then _____
         noun(s)   *had verbed.*   *noun would have verbed /or/ would verb*

Write four of your own sentences using this template. In some sentences use <u>if</u> instead of <u>I wish</u>.

1. _____

2. _____

3. _____

4 _____

Past Perfect Tense

PRACTICAL APPLICATION

Read the following short paragraph. <u>Underline</u> the verbs in past perfect. (Circle) the conditionals.

What a Mess!

It was 5:00 pm. I had finally come home after a hard day's work. I pulled out my key, unlocked the door, and stepped into the hallway. And what did I see? What a mess! It looked like a **tornado** had **swept** through every room. My husband clearly had had his friends over for a **poker** game. They'd left the playing cards **scattered** on the table and had left plates piled up in the sink. The news in the living room wasn't much better. The dog had decided he wanted to be a librarian. He had climbed up on the bookshelves and had **gnawed** on one of my books and had torn it to **shreds**. I put my hands over my eyes and walked into the bedroom. "I'll take a nap first," I said to myself, "and deal with this mess later." But what on earth had happened there? Madness! Chaos! **Jabberwocky**! Their were tree leaves **strewn** on the carpet and what looked like bird feathers! I suddenly realized that I had left the window open! A **mockingbird** had **fluttered** inside and was now peacefully **perched** on top of my dresser! "Out, out, out!" I said as I tried to **shoo** it away. He gave an angry **chirp** and flew out the open window. I shut it behind him. "What a disaster," I said. I wish I had stayed home today. Then this wouldn't have happened!" I lay down in bed and shut my eyes hoping that magically everything would be nice and clean by the time I woke up.

NOTES: Use this space to write notes about the usage of the tense.

---

tornado: whirlwind

sweep: blow

poker: card game

scattered: strewn

gnaw: chew

shreds: small pieces of paper or fabric

people-watch: look at people

Jabberwocky: chaos

strewn: scattered

mockingbird: gray and white bird

perch: sit like a bird or cat

shoo: chase

chirp: bird sound

Now you try! Write a paragraph in which you describe coming home and finding that things had changed in your absence...

Past Perfect Tense

Sentences In Past Perfect Tense

Level I

The red fox had eaten fruit before yesterday.
_____ had _____ before _____ .
     NP   VP Past Participle   time

Level II

The red fox had eaten fruit when he climbed up the apple tree.
_____ had _____ when _____ .
     NP   VP Past Participle   clause

Level III

The red fox had aleardy eaten ten apples when he climbed up the apple tree for mre.
_____ had already _____ when _____ .
     NP   VP Past Participle   clause

Note: Practice Pages utilize the generative rules introduced in the introduction to students section to encourage students to make as creative sentences as possible.

Simple Sentence
S → NP VP

Verb Phrase:
VP → (Adv) V (NP) (NP) (PP) (Adv)
VP → (Adv) V (VP) (PP) (Adv)

Noun Phrase:
NP → (Art) (Adj*) N (RC) (PP)

Adv = Adverb: *always, often, quickly, suddenly*
PP = Prepositional Phrase: *in, on, from*
Art = Article: *a, an, the*
Adj = Adjectives: *cute, fluffy, white*
RC = Relative Clause: the cat *that I saw at the shelter*

Parentheses () means optional
Asterick * means can have multiple

Past Perfect Tense

PRACTICE SENTENCES

1. _____
2. _____
3. _____

1. _____
2. _____
3. _____

1. _____
2. _____
3. _____

Notes: Use this space to note common mistakes, instances you can use the tense or anything that helps you use the tense.

Past Perfect Tense

QUESTIONS IN PAST PERFECT TENSE

LEVEL I

(Where)   had   the red fox   eaten fruit   before   yesterday?
(_____) had _____ _____ before _____ ?
   Wh-word   *NP*   *VP Past Participle*   *time*

LEVEL II

(Where)   had   the red fox   eaten fruit   before   he climbed the apple tree?
(_____) had _____ _____ before _____ ?
   Wh-word   *NP*   *VP Past Participle*   *clause*

LEVEL III

(Where)   had   the fruit   fallen   when   the fox woke up in the morning?
(_____) had _____ _____ when _____ ?
   Wh-word   *NP*   *VP Past Participle*   *clause*

Note: Practice Pages utilize the generative rules introduced in the introduction to students section to encourage students to make as creative sentences as possible.

Simple Sentence
S → NP VP

Verb Phrase:
VP → (Adv) V (NP) (NP) (PP) (Adv)
VP → (Adv) V (VP) (PP) (Adv)

Noun Phrase:
NP → (Art) (Adj*) N (RC) (PP)

Adv = Adverb: *always, often, quickly, suddenly*
PP = Prepositional Phrase: *in, on, from*
Art = Article: *a, an, the*
Adj = Adjectives: *cute, fluffy, white*
RC = Relative Clause: the cat *that I saw at the shelter*

Parentheses () means optional
Asterick * means can have multiple

120

Past Perfect Tense

PRACTICE SENTENCES

1. _____
   _____
2. _____
   _____
3. _____
   _____

1. _____
   _____
2. _____
   _____
3. _____
   _____

1. _____
   _____
2. _____
   _____
3. _____
   _____

Notes: Use this space to note common mistakes, instances you can use the tense or anything that helps you use the tense.

Past Perfect Tense

NEGATIVE STATEMENTS IN PAST PERFECT TENSE

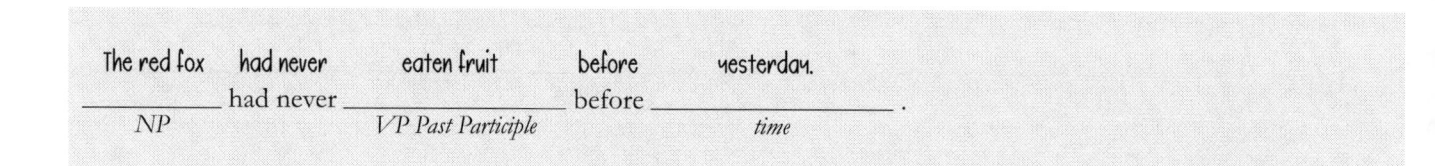

LEVEL I

The red fox had never eaten fruit before yesterday.
_____ had never _____ before _____ .
NP   VP Past Participle   time

LEVEL II

The red fox had never eaten fruit before he climbed up the apple tree.
_____ had never _____ before _____ .
NP   VP Past Participle   clause

LEVEL III

The red fox had never eaten fruit before it fell from the apple tree in the wind storm.
_____ had never _____ before _____ .
NP   VP Past Participle   clause

Note: Practice Pages utilize the generative rules introduced in the introduction to students section to encourage students to make as creative sentences as possible.

Simple Sentence
S → NP VP

Verb Phrase:
VP → (Adv) V (NP) (NP) (PP) (Adv)
VP → (Adv) V (VP) (PP) (Adv)

Noun Phrase:
NP → (Art) (Adj*) N (RC) (PP)

Adv = Adverb: *always, often, quickly, suddenly*
PP = Prepositional Phrase: *in, on, from*
Art = Article: *a, an, the*
Adj = Adjectives: *cute, fluffy, white*
RC = Relative Clause: the cat *that I saw at the shelter*

Parentheses () means optional
Asterick * means can have multiple

122

Past Perfect Tense

PRACTICE SENTENCES

1. _____
   _____
2. _____
   _____
3. _____
   _____

1. _____
   _____
2. _____
   _____
3. _____
   _____

1. _____
   _____
2. _____
   _____
3. _____
   _____

Notes: Use this space to note common mistakes, instances you can use the tense or anything that helps you use the tense.

Past Perfect Tense

MODAL STATEMENTS IN PAST PERFECT TENSE

LEVEL I

The red fox could have never eaten fruit before yesterday.

_____ could have never _____ before _____ .
     NP   VP Past Participle   time

LEVEL II

The red fox could have never eaten fruit until he climbed up the apple tree.

_____ could have never _____ before _____ .
     NP   VP Past Participle   clause

LEVEL III

The red fox ignored the fruit because he might have already eaten breakfast.

_____ because _____ might have already _____ .
    clause   NP   VP Past Participle

Note: Practice Pages utilize the generative rules introduced in the introduction to students section to encourage students to make as creative sentences as possible.

Simple Sentence
S → NP VP

Verb Phrase:
VP → (Adv) V (NP) (NP) (PP) (Adv)
VP → (Adv) V (VP) (PP) (Adv)

Noun Phrase:
NP → (Art) (Adj*) N (RC) (PP)

Adv = Adverb: *always, often, quickly, suddenly*
PP = Prepositional Phrase: *in, on, from*
Art = Article: *a, an, the*
Adj = Adjectives: *cute, fluffy, white*
RC = Relative Clause: the cat *that I saw at the shelter*

Parentheses () means optional
Asterick * means can have multiple

Past Perfect Tense

PRACTICE SENTENCES

1. _____
   _____
2. _____
   _____
3. _____
   _____

1. _____
   _____
2. _____
   _____
3. _____
   _____

1. _____
   _____
2. _____
   _____
3. _____
   _____

Notes: Use this space to note common mistakes, instances you can use the tense or anything that helps you use the tense.

Past Perfect Tense

NOUN CLAUSES IN PAST PERFECT TENSE

LEVEL I

I know	why	the red fox	had never	eaten fruit	before	yesterday.
Introductory Clause	wh-word	NP	had never	VP Past Participle	before	time

LEVEL II

I know	why	the red fox	had never	eaten fruit	before	he climbed up the apple tree
Introductory Clause	wh-word	NP	had never	VP Past Participle	before	time

LEVEL III

I know	why	the red fox ate the fruit	even though	he	had already	eaten breakfast.
Introductory Clause	wh-word	clause	even though	NP	had aleady	VP Past Participle

Note: Practice Pages utilize the generative rules introduced in the introduction to students section to encourage students to make as creative sentences as possible.

Simple Sentence
S → NP VP

Verb Phrase:
VP → (Adv) V (NP) (NP) (PP) (Adv)
VP → (Adv) V (VP) (PP) (Adv)

Noun Phrase:
NP → (Art) (Adj*) N (RC) (PP)

Adv = Adverb: *always, often, quickly, suddenly*
PP = Prepositional Phrase: *in, on, from*
Art = Article: *a, an, the*
Adj = Adjectives: *cute, fluffy, white*
RC = Relative Clause: the cat *that I saw at the shelter*

Parentheses () means optional
Asterick * means can have multiple

Past Perfect Tense

PRACTICE SENTENCES

1. _____
_____
2. _____
_____
3. _____
_____

1. _____
_____
2. _____
_____
3. _____
_____

1. _____
_____
2. _____
_____
3. _____
_____

Notes: Use this space to note common mistakes, instances you can use the tense or anything that helps you use the tense.

Past Perfect Progressive Tense

Rules

The past perfect progressive is used for:

* Duriations of actions which occured just before another action in the past
We <u>had been waiting</u> for an hour when the bus finally came.

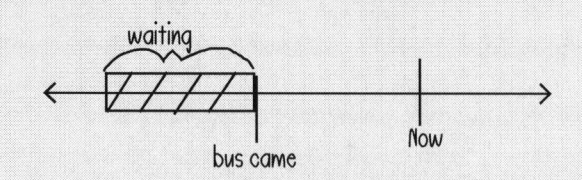

* Prior causes of something in the past
I missed you yesterday, because I <u>had been sleeping</u> when you came.

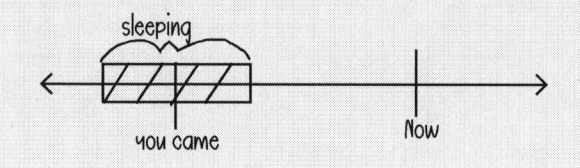

I.I Warm Up

Tell me about the things you <u>had been doing</u> before the following actions.

1. When the I woke up, <u>I had been dreaming for hours</u> about English.

2. When class ended,

3. When winter came,

4. When I got home,

5. When my friend came over,

Simple Past Perfect Progressive Tense Forms

I	had been	waiting	for an hour.
He She It	had been	waiting	
You We They	had been	waiting	

Negative Past Perfect Progressive Tense Forms

I	hadn't been	waiting	very long.
He She It	hadn't been	waiting	
You We They	hadn't been	waiting	

Yes-No Qs Past Perfect Progressive Tense Forms

Had	I	been waiting	very long?
Had	he she it	been waiting	
	you we they	been waiting	

Wh Qs Past Perfect Progressive Tense Forms

Where	had	I	been waiting?
Where	had	he she it	been waiting?
Where	had	you we they	been waiting?

Past Perfect Progressive Tense

Level I sentences

Duration prior to event in the past.

Level II sentences

Duration prior to event in the past + clause in simple past

Level III sentences

When + introductory clause + past perfect continous.

Level IV sentences

Duration + interution + multiple verbs

1. This morning, the snake <u>had been slithering</u> for hours.

_____ the _____ _____ for _____ .
  time word   *noun(s)*   *had been verbing*   *time*

2. <u>When the sun rose</u> this morning, the snake had been slithering for hours.

When _____ _____ _____
       adj + noun   *verbed*   *time word*

_____ _____ for _____ .
   noun   *had been verbing*   *time*

3. The snake had been slithering ever since the sun rose this morning.

_____ _____ ever since
   noun   *had been verbing*

_____ _____ _____ .
   noun   *verbed + obj*   *time word*

4. When the snake looked at the sky, he realized that the hawk had been circling for hours.

When _____ _____ _____ he realized
      noun   *verbed*   *object*

_____ _____ for _____ .
  noun   *had been verbing + obj*   *time*

5. The snake had been looking at the sky for hours when suddenly the hawk swooped down, snatched him, and ate him.

The _____ _____ for _____ when suddenly
     noun   *had been verbing*   *time*

_____ _____ _____
  noun   *verbed*   *object*

_____ and _____ .
   verbed + object   *verbed + object*

Past Perfect Progressive Tense

LET'S ASK SOME QUESTIONS

Asking questions in the past perfect progressive can be a bit tricky. Since the past perfect progressive often describes the relationship between two events, two clauses are required. These clauses are linked with "when" or "before" or "by the time that."

Example:

How long had you been studying English <u>when</u> you came to America?
(before/ by the time that)

How long had/ had	noun/ nouns	been verbing	object

by the time that/ when	noun/ nouns	verbed	object

1. _____
2. _____
3. _____
4. _____

> Since the past perfect progressive talks about duration of actions in the past, "how long" is the most common question form.
>
> Examples:
>
> *How long had you been waiting before I came?*
>
> *How long had you been sleeping before you woke up?*
>
> *How long had you been watching t.v. before you fell aslepp.*

NOW ANSWER WITH A NOUN CLAUSE

> Pick one of the introductory clauses below:
>
> It doesn't matter   I don't know   It's not important   It's not clear   I can't say

I don't know how long she had been waiting before she decided to leave.

Introductory clause	how long	noun(s)	had been verbing

before/ when/ by the time that	noun/ nouns	verbed	object

Write four answers to the questions above using an introductory clause.

1. _____
2. _____
3. _____
4. _____

> The past perfect progressive uses the regular subject verb object order following noun clauses.
>
> Examples:
>
> *I don't know how long she had been studying before she took the exam.*
>
> *It doesn't matter how long they had been dating before they got married.*
>
> *I can't tell you long I had been hoping for a new job by the time I finally got hired.*

Past Perfect Progressive Tense

CONDITIONS AND CONSEQUENCES

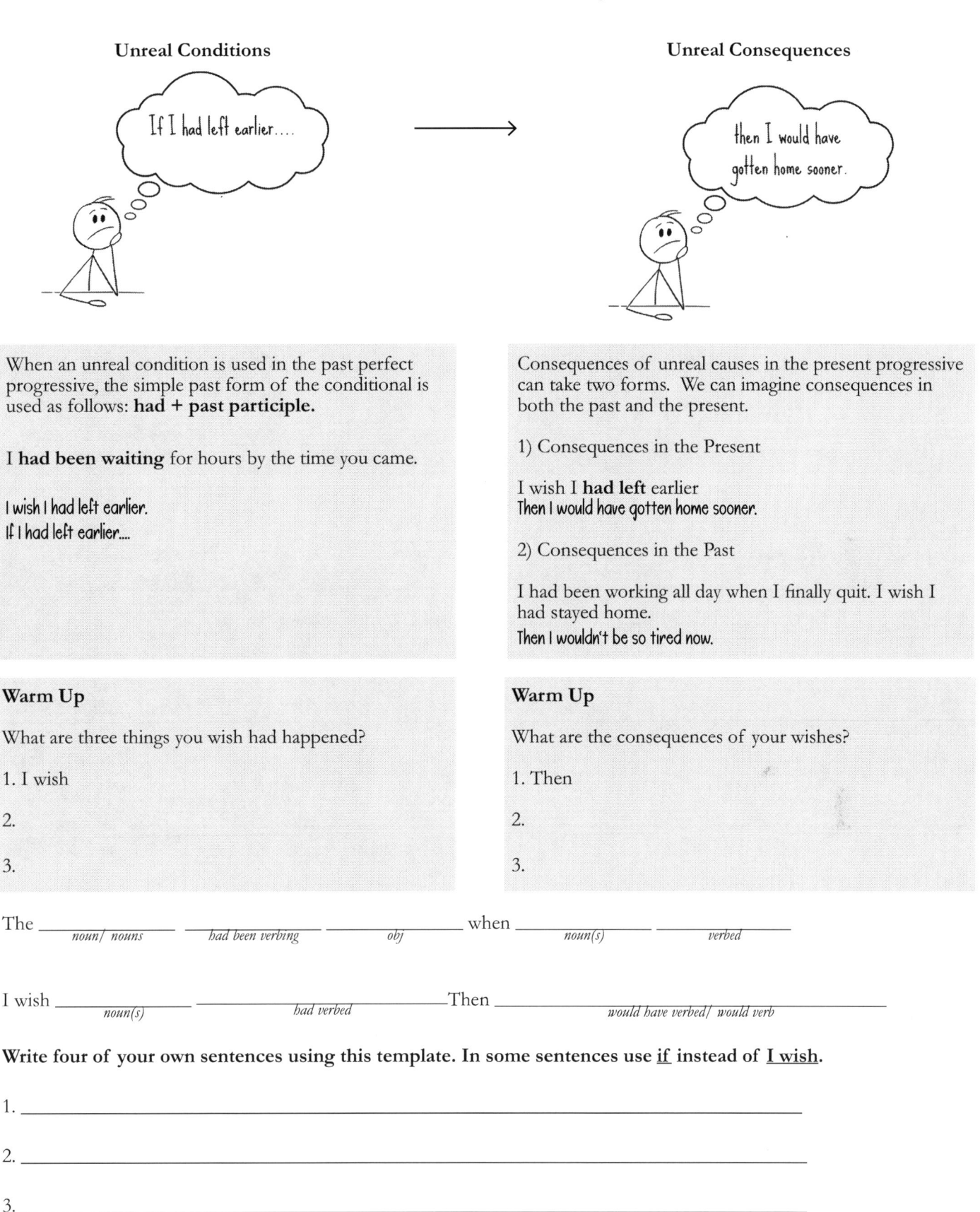

Unreal Conditions

(thought bubble: If I had left earlier....)

Unreal Consequences

(thought bubble: then I would have gotten home sooner.)

When an unreal condition is used in the past perfect progressive, the simple past form of the conditional is used as follows: **had + past participle.**

I **had been waiting** for hours by the time you came.

I wish I had left earlier.
If I had left earlier....

Consequences of unreal causes in the present progressive can take two forms. We can imagine consequences in both the past and the present.

1) Consequences in the Present

I wish I **had left** earlier
Then I would have gotten home sooner.

2) Consequences in the Past

I had been working all day when I finally quit. I wish I had stayed home.
Then I wouldn't be so tired now.

Warm Up

What are three things you wish had happened?

1. I wish

2.

3.

Warm Up

What are the consequences of your wishes?

1. Then

2.

3.

The _____ _____ _____ when _____ _____
     noun/ nouns   *had been verbing*   *obj*   *noun(s)*   *verbed*

I wish _____ _____ Then _____
     noun(s)   *had verbed*   *would have verbed/ would verb*

Write four of your own sentences using this template. In some sentences use <u>if</u> instead of <u>I wish</u>.

1. _____

2. _____

3. _____

4 _____

Past Perfect Progressive Tense

PRACTICAL APPLICATION

Read the following short paragraph. <u>Underline</u> the verbs in past perfect progressive. (Circle) the conditionals.

A Big Life Change

By the time I hit **the big 30**, I had really been **yearning** for a sense of purpose and fulfillment. The **daily ratrace** had been getting to me. I had been sitting in front of a computer **day in and day out**, working in a cubicle that felt like a prison. I had been **grinding my fingers to the bone** in a dead end job. I used to get up every morning and say, "This is **soul-sucking**! This is pure **monotony**! This a **quagmire** of **mediocrity**!" It had been an ongoing struggle just to drag myself along to my daily commute. This feeling of dissatisfaction had been building and building for some time. And, one day, it just **boiled over**. "That's it!" I said. "I'm throwing **caution to the wind**! I'm going to break out of this **rut** and chase my dreams!" That morning, I called my boss and **gave notice**. It was thanks to that decision that I feel that I've discovered my true calling as a circus acrobat. I only wish I had made the decision sooner. Then I would have spared myself a half-decade of corporate **doldrums**.

NOTES: Use this space to write notes about the usage of the tense.

---

the big 30: age 30

yearning: hoping

ratrace: work life

day in and day out: every day

grinding my fingers to the bone: working hard

soul-sucking: unfulfilling

monotony: boring

quagmire: swamp

mediocrity: 'meh'

boil over: reach a decisive moment

throw caution to the wind: take a chance

rut: boring routine

gave notice: quit

doldrums: boring period of time

Past Perfect Progressive Tense

Now you try! Write a paragraph in which you describe a decisive moment in your past. What <u>had been going on</u> before you made the big change?

SENTENCES IN PAST PEFFECT PROGRESSIVE TENSE

LEVEL I

The snake had been slithering for hours.

_____ had been _____ for _____.
NP   VP+ing   time

LEVEL II

The snake had been slithering when the sun rose.

_____ had been _____ when _____.
NP   VP+ing   clause +simple past

LEVEL III

The snake had been slithering ever since the sun rose this morning.

_____ had been _____ ever since _____.
NP   VP+ing   clause +simple past

Note: Practice Pages utilize the generative rules introduced in the introduction to students section to encourage students to make as creative sentences as possible.

Simple Sentence
S → NP VP

Verb Phrase:
VP → (Adv) V (NP) (NP) (PP) (Adv)
VP → (Adv) V (VP) (PP) (Adv)

Noun Phrase:
NP → (Art) (Adj*) N (RC) (PP)

Adv = Adverb: *always, often, quickly, suddenly*
PP = Prepositional Phrase: *in, on, from*
Art = Article: *a, an, the*
Adj = Adjectives: *cute, fluffy, white*
RC = Relative Clause: the cat *that I saw at the shelter*

Parentheses () means optional
Asterick * means can have multiple

Past Perfect Progressive Tense

PRACTICE SENTENCES

1. _____
   _____
2. _____
   _____
3. _____
   _____

1. _____
   _____
2. _____
   _____
3. _____
   _____

1. _____
   _____
2. _____
   _____
3. _____
   _____

Notes: Use this space to note common mistakes, instances you can use the tense or anything that helps you use the tense.

Past Perfect Progressive Tense

QUESTIONS IN PAST PERFECT PROGRESSIVE TENSE

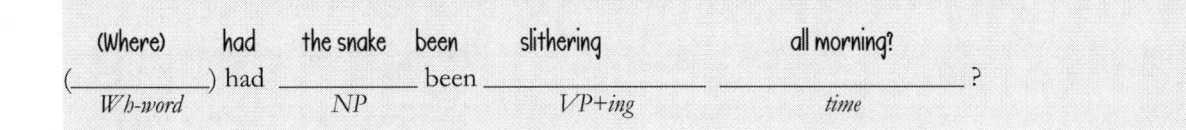

LEVEL I

(Where) had the snake been slithering all morning?
(_____) had _____ been _____ _____ ?
 Wh-word   *NP*   *VP+ing*   *time*

LEVEL II

(Where) had the snake been slithering when the sun rose?
(_____) had _____ been _____ when _____ ?
 Wh-word   *NP*   *VP+ing*   *clause+simple past*

LEVEL III

(Where) had the snake been slithering ever since it left its hole?
(_____) had _____ been _____ ever since _____ ?
 Wh-word   *NP*   *VP+ing*   *clause+simple past*

Note: Practice Pages utilize the generative rules introduced in the introduction to students section to encourage students to make as creative sentences as possible.

Simple Sentence
S → NP VP

Verb Phrase:
VP → (Adv) V (NP) (NP) (PP) (Adv)
VP → (Adv) V (VP) (PP) (Adv)

Noun Phrase:
NP → (Art) (Adj*) N (RC) (PP)

Adv = Adverb: *always, often, quickly, suddenly*
PP = Prepositional Phrase: *in, on, from*
Art = Article: *a, an, the*
Adj = Adjectives: *cute, fluffy, white*
RC = Relative Clause: the cat *that I saw at the shelter*

Parentheses () means optional
Asterick * means can have multiple

Past Perfect Progressive Tense

PRACTICE SENTENCES

1. _____
   _____
2. _____
   _____
3. _____
   _____

1. _____
   _____
2. _____
   _____
3. _____
   _____

1. _____
   _____
2. _____
   _____
3. _____
   _____

Notes: Use this space to note common mistakes, instances you can use the tense or anything that helps you use the tense.

Past Perfect Progressive Tense

NEGATIVE STATEMENTS IN PAST PERFECT PROGRESSIVE TENSE

LEVEL I

The snake hadn't been slithering for hours.

_____ hadn't been _____ for _____ .
NP / VP+ing / time

LEVEL II

The snake hadn't been slithering when the sun rose.

_____ hadn't been _____ when _____ .
NP / VP+ing / clause +simple past

LEVEL III

The snake hadn't been slithering ever since the sun rose this morning.

_____ hadn't been _____ ever since _____ .
NP / VP+ing / clause +simple past

Note: Practice Pages utilize the generative rules introduced in the introduction to students section to encourage students to make as creative sentences as possible.

Simple Sentence
S → NP VP

Verb Phrase:
VP → (Adv) V (NP) (NP) (PP) (Adv)
VP → (Adv) V (VP) (PP) (Adv)

Noun Phrase:
NP → (Art) (Adj*) N (RC) (PP)

Adv = Adverb: *always, often, quickly, suddenly*
PP = Prepositional Phrase: *in, on, from*
Art = Article: *a, an, the*
Adj = Adjectives: *cute, fluffy, white*
RC = Relative Clause: the cat *that I saw at the shelter*

Parentheses () means optional
Asterick * means can have multiple

Past Perfect Progressive Tense

PRACTICE SENTENCES

1. _____
_____
2. _____
_____
3. _____
_____

1. _____
_____
2. _____
_____
3. _____
_____

1. _____
_____
2. _____
_____
3. _____
_____

Notes: Use this space to note common mistakes, instances you can use the tense or anything that helps you use the tense.

Past Perfect Progressive Tense

MODAL STATEMENTS IN PAST PERFECT PROGRESSIVE TENSE

LEVEL I

The snake couldn't have been slithering for hours.

_____ couldn't have been _____ for _____ .
   NP   *VP+ing*   *time*

LEVEL II

The snake couldn't have been slithering when the sun rose.

_____ couldn't have been _____ when _____ .
   NP   *VP+ing*   *clause +simple past*

LEVEL III

The snake couldn't have been slithering ever since the sun rose this morning.

_____ couldn't have been _____ ever since _____ .
   NP   *VP+ing*   *clause +simple past*

Note: Practice Pages utilize the generative rules introduced in the introduction to students section to encourage students to make as creative sentences as possible.

Simple Sentence
S → NP VP

Verb Phrase:
VP → (Adv) V (NP) (NP) (PP) (Adv)
VP → (Adv) V (VP) (PP) (Adv)

Noun Phrase:
NP → (Art) (Adj*) N (RC) (PP)

Adv = Adverb: *always, often, quickly, suddenly*
PP = Prepositional Phrase: *in, on, from*
Art = Article: *a, an, the*
Adj = Adjectives: *cute, fluffy, white*
RC = Relative Clause: the cat *that I saw at the shelter*

Parentheses () means optional
Asterick * means can have multiple

140

Past Perfect Progressive Tense

PRACTICE SENTENCES

1. _____
2. _____
3. _____

1. _____
2. _____
3. _____

1. _____
2. _____
3. _____

Notes: Use this space to note common mistakes, instances you can use the tense or anything that helps you use the tense.

NOUN CLAUSES IN PAST PERFECT PROGRESSIVE TENSE

LEVEL I

I know	why	the snake	had been	slithering	for	hours.
Introductory Clause	wh-word	NP	had been / VP+ing		for / time	

LEVEL II

I know	why	the snake	had been	slithering	when	the sun rose.
Introductory Clause	wh-word	NP	had been / VP+ing		when / clause+ simple past	

LEVEL III

I know	why	the snake	had been	slithering	ever since	the sun rose this morning.
Introductory Clause	wh-word	NP	had been / VP+ing		ever sice / clause+ simple past	

Note: Practice Pages utilize the generative rules introduced in the introduction to students section to encourage students to make as creative sentences as possible.

Simple Sentence
S → NP VP

Verb Phrase:
VP → (Adv) V (NP) (NP) (PP) (Adv)
VP → (Adv) V (VP) (PP) (Adv)

Noun Phrase:
NP → (Art) (Adj*) N (RC) (PP)

Adv = Adverb: *always, often, quickly, suddenly*
PP = Prepositional Phrase: *in, on, from*
Art = Article: *a, an, the*
Adj = Adjectives: *cute, fluffy, white*
RC = Relative Clause: the cat *that I saw at the shelter*

Parentheses () means optional
Asterick * means can have multiple

Past Perfect Progressive Tense

PRACTICE SENTENCES

1. _____
_____
2. _____
_____
3. _____
_____

1. _____
_____
2. _____
_____
3. _____
_____

1. _____
_____
2. _____
_____
3. _____
_____

Notes: Use this space to note common mistakes, instances you can use the tense or anything that helps you use the tense.

Simple Future Tense

Rules

The simple future is used for:

* **Plans (going to only)**
This weekend, I'm going to go to the zoo.

* **Predictions (either will or going to)**
I think it will rain tomorrow.

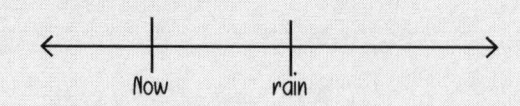

```
<———|————|————>
    Now  rain
```

*** Consequences (will)**
If you eat too much, you will feel sick.

* **Promises and favors**
I will help you with your homework.

1.1 Warm Up

This weekend,

1. I'm going to clean the house.

2.

3.

If it rains,

1. We will get wet.

2.

3.

Tomorrow, I think

1. My parents will call me.

2.

3.

Simple Future Tense Forms

I	will	work	tomorrow.

He She It	will	work	

You We They	will	work	

Negative Future Tense Forms

I	won't	work	tomorrow.

He She It	won't	work	

You We They	won't	work	

Yes-No Qs Future Tense Forms

Will	I	work	tomorrow?

Will	he she it	work	

Will	you we they	work	

Wh Qs Future Tense Forms

Where	will	I	work	tomorrow?

Where	will	he she it	work	

Where	will	you we they	work	

Level I sentences

One clause + time word

1. The goat will eat grass tomorrow.

The _____ _____ _____
　　　noun(s)　　　　　will/ is going to verb + object　　time word

2. Tomorrow the goat will eat grass.

_____ the _____ _____
time word　　　　　noun　　　　will/ is going to verb + object

Level II sentences

+ prepositional phrase

3. Tomorrow the goat with the curly horns will eat grass.

_____ the _____ with the _____ _____
time word　　　　noun　　　　　　　adj + noun(s)　　will/ is going to verb + object

4. The goat with the curly horns will eat grass tomorrow.

The _____ with the _____ _____ _____
　　　noun　　　　　　　adj + noun　　will/ is going to verb + object　　time word

Level III sentences

+ prepositional phrase
subject adjective clause

5. The goat that <u>lives at the farm</u> will eat grass tomorrow.

The _____ _____ _____
　　　noun　　　who/that　　verbs + object

_____ _____
will/ is going to verb + object　　time word

Level IV sentences

+ prepositional phrase
+ object adjective clause

6. The goat <u>that we see everyday</u> will eat grass tomorrow.

The _____ _____ _____ _____
　　　noun　　　who/that　　noun　　　verbs + object

_____ _____
will/ is going to verb + object　　time word

7. The goat with the curly horns <u>that we see everyday</u> will eat grass tomorrow.

The _____ with the _____ _____ _____
　　　noun　　　　　　adj + noun　　who/ that/ which　　noun

_____ _____ _____
verb(s) + object　　will/ is going to verb + object　　time word

145

Simple Future Tense

LET'S ASK SOME QUESTIONS

Take a couple of your sentences from the previous page. Write four questions. Use the yes/no form or a "wh-word."

Example:

Will the goat eat grass tomorrow? Is the goat going to eat grass tomorrow?
When will the goat eat grass tomorrow? When is the goat going to eat grass tomorrow?

_____ _____ _____ _____
Will/ When will   *noun/ nouns*   *verb*   *object + time word*

_____ _____ _____ _____
Is/ When is   *noun/ nouns*   *going to verb*   *object + time word*

1. _____
2. _____
3. _____
4. _____

NOW ANSWER WITH A NOUN CLAUSE

> Pick one of the introductory clauses below:
>
> It doesn't matter   I don't know   It's not important   It's not clear   I can't say

I don't know <u>whether or not</u> the goat will eat grass tomorrow.
            (if)
It doesn't matter <u>when</u> the goat is going to eat grass tomorrow.

_____ _____ _____ _____
Introductory clause   *whethe or not/ if/ wh-word*   *noun(s)*   *will verb*

Write four answers to the questions above using an introductory clause.

1. _____
2. _____
3. _____
4. _____

The simple future talks about plans, predictions, and quick decisions. "When" is the most common wh-word.

Examples:

Will you leave?

When will they arrive?

How will they do that?

Who will she give the letter to?

Where will they put the book?

When yes/ no questions become noun-clauses they take *if* or *whether or not.*

Examples:

I don't know if the goat will eat grass.

It doesn't matter whether or not the goat will eat grass.

I can't say whether or not the goat will eat grass.

Simple Future Tense

CONDITIONS AND CONSEQUENCES

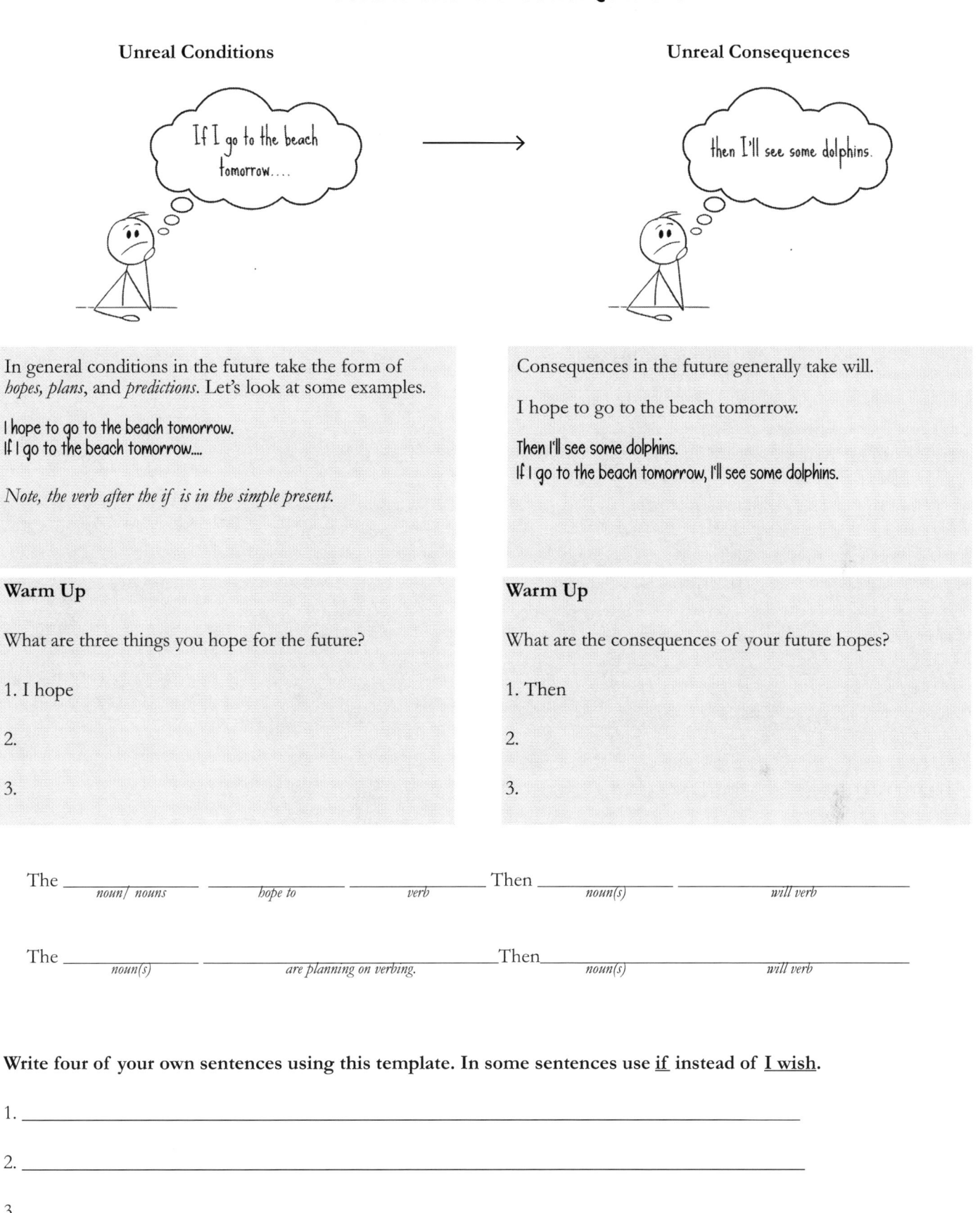

Unreal Conditions

If I go to the beach tomorrow....

Unreal Consequences

then I'll see some dolphins.

In general conditions in the future take the form of *hopes*, *plans*, and *predictions*. Let's look at some examples.

I hope to go to the beach tomorrow.
If I go to the beach tomorrow....

Note, the verb after the if is in the simple present.

Consequences in the future generally take will.

I hope to go to the beach tomorrow.

Then I'll see some dolphins.
If I go to the beach tomorrow, I'll see some dolphins.

Warm Up

What are three things you hope for the future?

1. I hope

2.

3.

Warm Up

What are the consequences of your future hopes?

1. Then

2.

3.

The _____ _____ _____ Then _____ _____
     noun/ nouns   *hope to*   *verb*   *noun(s)*   *will verb*

The _____ _____ Then _____ _____
     noun(s)   *are planning on verbing.*   *noun(s)*   *will verb*

Write four of your own sentences using this template. In some sentences use <u>if</u> instead of <u>I wish</u>.

1. _____

2. _____

3. _____

4 _____

PRACTICAL APPLICATION

Read the following short paragraph. <u>Underline</u> the verbs in simple future tense.

A Fantastic Getaway

I'm planning on taking a fantastic vacation. It'll be four weeks in paradise in **scenic** Black Canyon City. They have the best pies in Arizona: **boysenberry, gooseberry,** and **rhubarb**. As I drive down the highway, the warm desert breeze will **ruffle** my hair. Wide open spaces will **stretch out** toward the horizon in every direction. I can't say that I'll stay in a fancy hotel. I'm planning on bringing a tent with me and **pitching** it in the middle of the wilderness. My friends say that I'll hear coyotes **howling** from the mountains. That'll be a little scary, but I hear that they rarely attack humans. During the day, I'll **backpack** through the famous trails of Mojave. I'll see waterfalls **cascading** down the mountains. I'll see **saguaro** cactuses branching off into the sky. I'll see gigantic vultures circling in the air. It'll be breathtaking. And what will I do after a day of taking in such majestic sights? Why, eat one slice of pie after another!

NOTES: Use this space to write notes about the usage of this tense.

Getaway: vacation

boysenberry, gooseberry, rhubarb: kinds of pies

ruffle: whip

stretch out: extend

pitch a tent: set up a tent

howl: loud, animal cry

backpack: hike

cascade: fall (as a waterfall)

saguaro: giant cactus

magestic: amazing

Now you try! Write a paragraph in which you describe a future plan. What will you do? What will you see? What will you hear?

Simple Future Tense

SENTENCES IN SIMPLE FUTURE

LEVEL I

The goat	will	eat grass	tomorrow
NP	will	VP	time word

LEVEL II

The goat	with	the curly horns	will	eat grass	tomorrow
NP	with	NP	will	VP	time word

LEVEL III

The goat	that	lives on the farm	will	eat grass	tomorrow
NP	that	RC	will	VP	time word

Note: Practice Pages utilize the generative rules introduced in the introduction to students section to encourage students to make as creative sentences as possible.

Simple Sentence
S → NP VP

Verb Phrase:
VP → (Adv) V (NP) (NP) (PP) (Adv)
VP → (Adv) V (VP) (PP) (Adv)

Noun Phrase:
NP → (Art) (Adj*) N (RC) (PP)

Adv = Adverb: *always, often, quickly, suddenly*
PP = Prepositional Phrase: *in, on, from*
Art = Article: *a, an, the*
Adj = Adjectives: *cute, fluffy, white*
RC = Relative Clause: the cat *that I saw at the shelter*

Parentheses () means optional
Asterick * means can have multiple

Practice Sentences

Simple Future Tense

1. _____
2. _____
3. _____

1. _____
2. _____
3. _____

1. _____
2. _____
3. _____

Notes: Use this space to note common mistakes, instances you can use the tense or anything that helps you use the tense.

Simple Future Tense

QUESTIONS IN FUTURE SIMPLE TENSE

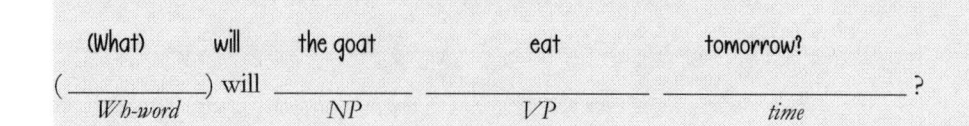

LEVEL I

(What)   will   the goat   eat   tomorrow?
(_____) will _____ _____ _____?
 Wh-word   NP   VP   time

LEVEL II

(What)   will   the goat   with   the curly horns   eat   tomorrow?
(_____) will _____ with _____ _____ _____?
 Wh-word   NP   NP   VP   time

LEVEL III

(What)   will   the goat   that   lives on the farm   eat   tomorrow?
(_____) will _____ that _____ _____ _____?
 Wh-word   NP   RC   VP   time

Note: Practice Pages utilize the generative rules introduced in the introduction to students section to encourage students to make as creative sentences as possible.

Simple Sentence
S → NP VP

Verb Phrase:
VP → (Adv) V (NP) (NP) (PP) (Adv)
VP → (Adv) V (VP) (PP) (Adv)

Noun Phrase:
NP → (Art) (Adj*) N (RC) (PP)

Adv = Adverb: *always, often, quickly, suddenly*
PP = Prepositional Phrase: *in, on, from*
Art = Article: *a, an, the*
Adj = Adjectives: *cute, fluffy, white*
RC = Relative Clause: the cat *that I saw at the shelter*

Parentheses () means optional
Asterick * means can have multiple

Simple Future Tense

PRACTICE SENTENCES

1. _____
_____
2. _____
_____
3. _____
_____

1. _____
_____
2. _____
_____
3. _____
_____

1. _____
_____
2. _____
_____
3. _____
_____

Notes: Use this space to note common mistakes, instances you can use the tense or anything that helps you use the tense.

Simple Future Tense

NEGATIVE STATEMENTS IN SIMPLE FUTURE TENSE

LEVEL I

The goat — won't — eat grass — tomorrow
_____ won't _____ _____ .
NP　　　　　　　　　VP　　　　time word

LEVEL II

The goat — with — the curly horns — won't — eat grass — tomorrow
_____ with _____ won't _____ _____ .
NP　　　　　NP　　　　　　VP　　　time word

LEVEL III

The goat — that — lives on the farm — won't — eat grass — tomorrow
_____ that _____ won't _____ _____ .
NP　　　　RC　　　　　　　VP　　　time word

Note: Practice Pages utilize the generative rules introduced in the introduction to students section to encourage students to make as creative sentences as possible.

Simple Sentence
S → NP VP

Verb Phrase:
VP → (Adv) V (NP) (NP) (PP) (Adv)
VP → (Adv) V (VP) (PP) (Adv)

Noun Phrase:
NP → (Art) (Adj*) N (RC) (PP)

Adv = Adverb: *always, often, quickly, suddenly*
PP = Prepositional Phrase: *in, on, from*
Art = Article: *a, an, the*
Adj = Adjectives: *cute, fluffy, white*
RC = Relative Clause: the cat *that I saw at the shelter*

Parentheses () means optional
Asterick * means can have multiple

Simple Future Tense

PRACTICE SENTENCES

1. _____
_____
2. _____
_____
3. _____
_____

1. _____
_____
2. _____
_____
3. _____
_____

1. _____
_____
2. _____
_____
3. _____
_____

Notes: Use this space to note common mistakes, instances you can use the tense or anything that helps you use the tense.

Simple Future Tense

NOUN CLAUSES IN SIMPLE FUTURE TENSE

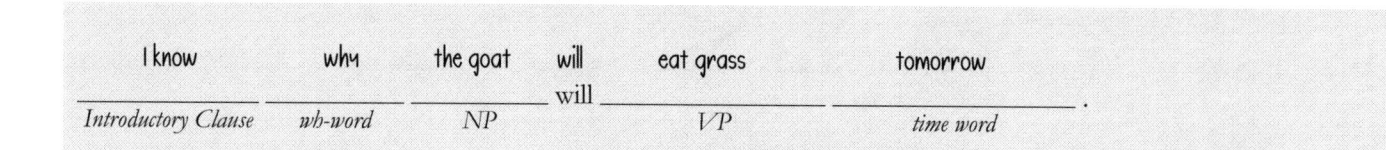

LEVEL I

I know	why	the goat	will	eat grass	tomorrow
Introductory Clause	wh-word	NP	will	VP	time word

LEVEL II

I know	why	the goat	with	the curly horns	will	eat grass	tomorrow
Introductory Clause	wh-word	NP	with	NP	will	VP	time word

LEVEL III

I know	why	the goat	that	lives on a farm	will	eat grass	tomorrow
Introductory Clause	wh-word	NP	that	RC	will	VP	time word

Note: Practice Pages utilize the generative rules introduced in the introduction to students section to encourage students to make as creative sentences as possible.

Simple Sentence
S → NP VP

Verb Phrase:
VP → (Adv) V (NP) (NP) (PP) (Adv)
VP → (Adv) V (VP) (PP) (Adv)

Noun Phrase:
NP → (Art) (Adj*) N (RC) (PP)

Adv = Adverb: *always, often, quickly, suddenly*
PP = Prepositional Phrase: *in, on, from*
Art = Article: *a, an, the*
Adj = Adjectives: *cute, fluffy, white*
RC = Relative Clause: the cat *that I saw at the shelter*

Parentheses () means optional
Asterick * means can have multiple

Simple Future Tense

PRACTICE SENTENCES

1. _____
   _____
2. _____
   _____
3. _____
   _____

1. _____
   _____
2. _____
   _____
3. _____
   _____

1. _____
   _____
2. _____
   _____
3. _____
   _____

Notes: Use this space to note common mistakes, instances you can use the tense or anything that helps you use the tense.

Future Progressive Tense

Rules

The future progressive is used for:

* **Actions in progress at a specific time in the future**
At 1:00 tomorrow, the birds will be singing.

* **Actions interrupted in the future**
I will be sleeping when you come home.

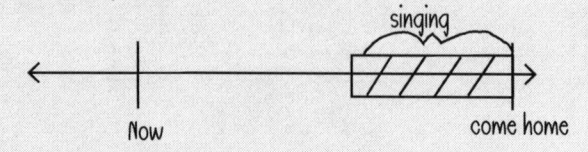

* **Simultaneous actions in the future**
Tomorrow, while the sun is shining, the birds will be singing.

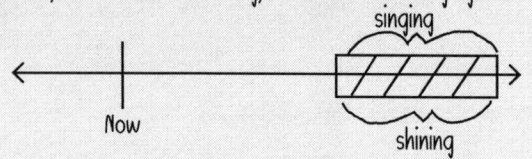

I.I Warm Up

What will be happening tomorrow night?

1. Tomorrow night, the stars will be shining.

2.

3.

What will you be doing when I come home?

1. I will be sleeping when you come home.

2.

3.

What will your friends and family be doing at this time tomorrow?

1. My brother will be studying. My father...

2.

Simple Future Progressive Tense Forms

I	will be	working	tomorrow.
He She It	will be	working	
You We They	will be	working	

Negative Future Progressive Tense Forms

I	won't be	working	tomorrow.
He She It	won't be	working	
You We They	won't be	working	

Yes-No Qs Future Progressive Tense Forms

Will	I	be working	tomorrow?
Will	he she it	be working	
Will	you we they	be working	

Wh Qs Future Progessive Tense Forms

Where	will	I	be working	tomorrow?
Where	will	he she it	be working	
Where	will	you we they	be working	

Future Progressive Tense

Level I sentences

Time word (*Yesterday, this morning, last night*) and one clause.

Add an object

Level II sentences

Simultaneous action, linked with "while."

Note present progressive

Level III sentences

Add an interruption in simple future

Level IV sentences

Add as second clause.

1. <u>Tomorrow</u>, the hungry cow will be eating.

_____ the _____ _____ _____
Specific time   *adjective*   *noun(s)*   *will be verbing*

2. <u>Tomorrow</u>, the hungry cow will be eating green grass.

_____ the _____ _____ _____.
specific time   *adj noun*   *will be verbing*   *object*

3. <u>While</u> the hungry cow <u>is eating</u> green grass, the horse <u>will be eating</u> hay.

Tomorrow while the _____ _____ _____ _____
                     adjective   *noun*   *is verbing*   *obj*

_____ _____ _____.
adj noun   *will be verbing*   *object*

4. Tomorrow the hungry cow will be eating green grass, when suddenly the farmer will run from the house.

Tomorrow the _____ _____ _____ _____ when suddenly
            adjective *noun(s)* *will be verbing* *object*

_____ _____.
adj noun   *will verb + object*

5. Tomorrow the hungry cow will be eating green grass and the horse will be eating hay, when suddenly the farmer will run from the house and chase the crows.

Tomorrow the _____ _____ _____ _____
            adjective *noun(s)* *will be verbing* *object*

and the _____ _____ _____ _____ when suddenly
       adjective *noun(s)* *will be verbing* *object*

the _____ _____ and _____ _____.
   adj noun *will verb*   *verb*   *object*

Future Progressive Tense

LET'S ASK SOME QUESTIONS

Take a couple of your sentences from the previous page. Write four questions. Use the yes/no form or "when"

Example:

Will the cow be eating grass tomorrow?
When will the cow be eating grass?

_____ _____ _____ _____
  Will   *noun/ nouns* *be verbing*   *object/ time word*

_____ _____ _____ _____
 When will *noun/ nouns* *be verbing*   *object*

1. _____

2. _____

3. _____

4. _____

> Future progressive talks about what will be in progress (unfinished) at a moment in the future. Questions often start with "Will" or "when."
>
> Examples:
>
> *Will you be sleeping when I get home?*
>
> *When will you be studying?*
>
> *Will you be eating dinner when I call?*

NOW ANSWER WITH A NOUN CLAUSE

Pick one of the introductory clauses below:
It doesn't matter   I don't know   It's not important   It's not clear   I can't say

I don't know <u>whether or not</u> the cow will be eating grass.
    (if)
It doesn't matter <u>when</u> the cow will be eating grass.

_____ _____ _____ _____
Introductory clause *whether or not/ if/ why* *noun(s)* *will be verbing*

_____ _____ _____ _____
Introductory clause   *when*   *noun/ nouns* *will be verbing*

Write four answers to the questions above using an introductory clause.

1. _____

2. _____

3. _____

4. _____

> When yes/ no questions become noun-clauses they take *if* or *whether or not.*
>
> Examples:
>
> *I don't know if I'll be sleeping when you call.*
>
> *It doesn't matter whether or not I'll be sleeping.*
>
> *I can't say when I'll be sleeping.*

Future Progressive Tense

CONDITIONS AND CONSEQUENCES

Unreal Conditions

If the sun is shining tomorrow...

→

Unreal Consequences

then I'll play soccer.

Usually the future progressive stays roughly the same in conditional forms.

I hope the sun will be shining tomorrow.
If the sun is shining tomorrow...

In general, consequences of this condition are in the simple future.

I hope the sun will be shining tomorrow.
Then I'll play soccer.
If the sun is shining tomorrow, I'll play soccer.

Warm Up

What are three things you hope will be happening?

1. I hope

2.

3.

Warm Up

What are the consequences of your hopes?

1. Then

2.

3.

I hope _____ _____ _____ Then _____ _____
　　　　noun/ nouns　　*will be verbing*　　*time*　　　　　*noun(s)*　　*will verb*

Write four of your own sentences using this template. In some sentences use <u>if</u> instead of <u>I wish</u>.

1. _____

2. _____

3. _____

4 _____

Future Progressive Tense

PRACTICAL APPLICATION

Read the following short paragraph. Underline the verbs in future progressive tense. (Circle) the simple future.

As soon as work is over...

When the clock **strikes** five this afternoon, I'll be dancing for joy. The work week will be over and I'll be looking forward to Friday night. I can see it now! I'll **swing** into the driveway, **skip** my way up the sidewalk, open the door, and then ah! Relaxation! My husband will be cooking dinner: **stir-frying** vegetables, and stirring a nice, thick, creamy pot of soup. The scent of **cloves** and cinnamon will be **wafting** through the house. Gentle music will be playing in the living room: cool jazz or classical. And my dogs! They'll be so happy to see me. By the time they hear the car door shut, they'll be barking and **wagging** their tails. When they hear me coming up the drive, their little paws will be **scraping** the door in anticipation. Dogs are wonderful, aren't they? Hello Laughter! Hello Sneakers, I'll say, and ruffle their ears. After dinner, we'll be **couch-potatoes** for the rest of the evening. We'll just sprawl on the cushions and watch Netflix. We're really getting into this series, and I can't wait to find out what heppens next. Oh! They say that there's a snowstorm coming tonight. So maybe, while the t.v. **flickers** in our **cozy den**, we'll get to see the fat flakes falling in the yard. Maybe, by morning, we'll have a **winter wonderland** to look forward to. Yes, it'll be a lovely evening. Only two more hours to go!

NOTES:

---

strike: to reach an hour

swing: turn

skip: run playfully

stir-fry: cook vegetables in a frying pan.

cloves: spices

waft: drift

wag tail: the way a dog moves its tail back and forth

scrape: scratch.

couch potato: lazy person

flicker: the way light dances on and off

cozy: comfortable

den: home

winter wonderland: snowy landscape

Now you try! Write a paragraph in which you imagine <u>what will be happening</u> when you get home?

Future Progressive Tense

SENTENCES IN FUTURE PROGRESSIVE TENSE

LEVEL I

The cow | will be | eating grass | tomorrow.
_____ will be _____ _____.
NP | | VP | *time word*

LEVEL II

The cow | will be | eating grass | while | the horse is eating hay.
_____ will be _____ while _____.
NP | | VP | | *clause present progressive*

LEVEL III

The cow | will be | eating grass | when suddenly | the farmer will run out of the barn.
_____ will be _____ when suddenly _____.
NP | | VP | | *clause present progressive*

Note: Practice Pages utilize the generative rules introduced in the introduction to students section to encourage students to make as creative sentences as possible.

Simple Sentence
S → NP VP

Verb Phrase:
VP → (Adv) V (NP) (NP) (PP) (Adv)
VP → (Adv) V (VP) (PP) (Adv)

Noun Phrase:
NP → (Art) (Adj*) N (RC) (PP)

Adv = Adverb: *always, often, quickly, suddenly*
PP = Prepositional Phrase: *in, on, from*
Art = Article: *a, an, the*
Adj = Adjectives: *cute, fluffy, white*
RC = Relative Clause: the cat *that I saw at the shelter*

Parentheses () means optional
Asterick * means can have multiple

Future Progressive Tense

PRACTICE SENTENCES

1. _____
2. _____
3. _____

1. _____
2. _____
3. _____

1. _____
2. _____
3. _____

Notes: Use this space to note common mistakes, instances you can use the tense or anything that helps you use the tense.

Future Progressive Tense

QUESTIONS IN FUTURE PROGRESSIVE TENSE

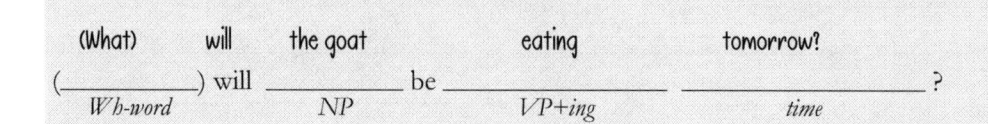

LEVEL I

(What) will the goat be eating tomorrow?
(_____) will _____ be _____ _____ ?
  Wh-word   NP   VP+ing   time

LEVEL II

(What) will the cow be eating while the horse is eating hay?
(_____) will _____ be _____ while _____ ?
  Wh-word   NP   VP   clause +present progressive

LEVEL III

(What) will the cow be eating when suddenly the farmer runs from the barn?
(_____) will _____ be _____ when suddenly _____ ?
  Wh-word   NP   VP   clause +simple present

Note: Practice Pages utilize the generative rules introduced in the introduction to students section to encourage students to make as creative sentences as possible.

Simple Sentence
S → NP VP

Verb Phrase:
VP → (Adv) V (NP) (NP) (PP) (Adv)
VP → (Adv) V (VP) (PP) (Adv)

Noun Phrase:
NP → (Art) (Adj*) N (RC) (PP)

Adv = Adverb: *always, often, quickly, suddenly*
PP = Prepositional Phrase: *in, on, from*
Art = Article: *a, an, the*
Adj = Adjectives: *cute, fluffy, white*
RC = Relative Clause: the cat *that I saw at the shelter*

Parentheses () means optional
Asterick * means can have multiple

Practice Sentences

Future Progressive Tense

1. _____
2. _____
3. _____

1. _____
2. _____
3. _____

1. _____
2. _____
3. _____

Notes: Use this space to note common mistakes, instances you can use the tense or anything that helps you use the tense.

Future Progressive Tense

NEGATIVE STATEMENTS IN FUTURE PROGRESSIVE TENSE

LEVEL I

The cow — won't be — eating grass — tomorrow.
_____ won't be _____ _____ .
   NP   VP   time word

LEVEL II

The cow — won't be — eating grass — while — the horse is eating hay.
_____ won't be _____ while _____ .
   NP   VP   clause present progressive

LEVEL III

The cow — won't be — eating grass — when — the farmer opens the barn door .
_____ won't be _____ when _____ .
   NP   VP   clause simple present

Note: Practice Pages utilize the generative rules introduced in the introduction to students section to encourage students to make as creative sentences as possible.

Simple Sentence
S → NP VP

Verb Phrase:
VP → (Adv) V (NP) (NP) (PP) (Adv)
VP → (Adv) V (VP) (PP) (Adv)

Noun Phrase:
NP → (Art) (Adj*) N (RC) (PP)

Adv = Adverb: *always, often, quickly, suddenly*
PP = Prepositional Phrase: *in, on, from*
Art = Article: *a, an, the*
Adj = Adjectives: *cute, fluffy, white*
RC = Relative Clause: the cat *that I saw at the shelter*

Parentheses () means optional
Asterick * means can have multiple

Future Progressive Tense

PRACTICE SENTENCES

1. _____
_____
2. _____
_____
3. _____
_____

1. _____
_____
2. _____
_____
3. _____
_____

1. _____
_____
2. _____
_____
3. _____
_____

Notes: Use this space to note common mistakes, instances you can use the tense or anything that helps you use the tense.

Future Progressive Tense

NOUN CLAUSES IN FUTURE PROGRESSIVE TENSE

LEVEL I

I know | why | the goat | will be | eating grass | tomorrow
_____ | _____ | _____ will be _____ | _____ | _____.
Introductory Clause | *wh-word* | *NP* | *VP* | *time word*

LEVEL II

I know | why | the goat | will be | eating grass | while | the horse is eating hay.
_____ | _____ | _____ will be _____ | _____ while _____.
Introductory Clause | *wh-word* | *NP* | *VP* | *clause+present progressive*

LEVEL III

I know | why | the goat | will be | eating grass | when | the farmer runs out of the barn | suddenly.
_____ | _____ | _____ will be _____ | _____ when _____ suddenly.
Introductory Clause | *wh-word* | *NP* | *VP* | *clause+simple future*

Note: Practice Pages utilize the generative rules introduced in the introduction to students section to encourage students to make as creative sentences as possible.

Simple Sentence
S → NP VP

Verb Phrase:
VP → (Adv) V (NP) (NP) (PP) (Adv)
VP → (Adv) V (VP) (PP) (Adv)

Noun Phrase:
NP → (Art) (Adj*) N (RC) (PP)

Adv = Adverb: *always, often, quickly, suddenly*
PP = Prepositional Phrase: *in, on, from*
Art = Article: *a, an, the*
Adj = Adjectives: *cute, fluffy, white*
RC = Relative Clause: the cat *that I saw at the shelter*

Parentheses () means optional
Asterick * means can have multiple

Future Progressive Tense

PRACTICE SENTENCES

1. _____
   _____
2. _____
   _____
3. _____
   _____

1. _____
   _____
2. _____
   _____
3. _____
   _____

1. _____
   _____
2. _____
   _____
3. _____
   _____

Notes: Use this space to note common mistakes, instances you can use the tense or anything that helps you use the tense.

Future Perfect Tense

Rules

The future perfect is used for:

* Actions which happened before another action in the future (often with "just" or "already")
By 6:00 tomorrow, I will have just woken up.
By the time that I leave, I will have already eaten lunch.

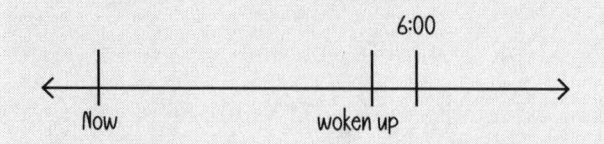

* Duration before another action in the future
By the time I leave, I will have lived here for ten years.

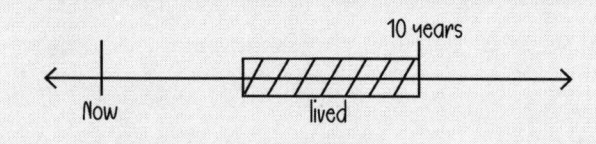

1.1 Warm Up

Talk about the things that you will have done, by the time you turn ninety.

1. By the time I turn 90, I will have learned English.
2.
3.
4.
5.

Simple Future Perfect Tense Forms

I	will have	already	eaten.
He She It	will have		eaten.
You We They	will be		eaten.

Negative Future Perfect Tense Forms

I	won't have	eaten	yet
He She It	won't have	eaten	
You We They	won't have	eaten	

Yes-No Qs Future Perfect Tense Forms

Will	I	have eaten	yet?
Will	he she it	have eaten	
Will	you we they	have eaten	

Wh Qs Future Perfect Forms

Where	will	I	have eaten	?
Where	will	he she it	have eaten	
Where	will	you we they	have eaten	

Future Perfect Tense

Level I sentences

Actions completed by a future point.

1. **By tomorrow, the dophin will have swum home.**

By _____ the _____ _____.
    time   *noun*   *will have verbed + object*

Level II sentences

Actions completed by a future point indicated by "by the time"

2. <u>By the time the sun sets tomorrow,</u> the dophin will have swum home.

By the time _____ _____ tommorow
              noun   *verbs + object*

_____ _____ _____.
  noun   *will have verbed*   *object*

Level III sentences

+ multiple verbs

3. By the time the sun sets tomorrow, the dolphin will have swum home and gone to sleep.

By the time _____ _____ tommorow
              noun   *verbs + object*

_____ _____ and _____.
  noun   *will have verbed+ object*   *verbed + object*

4. Tomorrow, by the time the sun sets, the dolphin will have swum home and gone to sleep.

Tomorrow, by the time _____ _____
                        noun   *verbs + object*

_____ _____ and _____.
  noun   *will have verbed+ object*   *verbed + object*

Level IV sentences

Muliple clauses in both simple present and future perfect

5. Tomorrow, by the time the sun sets and the moon comes out, the dolphin will have swum home and gone to sleep.

Tomorrow, by the time _____ _____
                        noun   *verbs + object*

and _____ _____
      noun   *verbs + object*

_____ _____ and _____.
  noun   *will have verbed+ object*   *verbed + object*

173

Future Perfect Tense

LET'S ASK SOME QUESTIONS

Asking questions in future perfect and progressive can be a bit tricky. Usually it will involve multiple clauses linked with "when" or "before" or "by the time that."

Example:

How long will you have studied English <u>when</u> you graduate college?
(by the time that)

_____ _____ _____ _____
How long will   *noun/ nouns*   *have verbed*   *object*

_____ _____ _____ _____
by the time that/ when   *noun/ nouns*   *verb*   *object*

1. _____
2. _____
3. _____
4. _____

Will you have already gone to sleep by the time I get home this evening?
(when)

_____ _____ _____ _____
Will noun have   *already*   *verbed*   *by the time that*

_____ _____ _____ _____
noun   *verbs*   *object*   *time word*

1. _____
2. _____
3. _____
4. _____

Since the future perfect talks about duration of actions in the future, "how long" is the most common question form.

Examples:

How long will you have studied English when you graduate?

How long will you have slept before you wake up tomorrow?

How long will you have watched TV before you go to bed tonight?

The future perfect uses the regular subject verb object order following noun clauses.

Examples:

I don't know how long she will have studied before she takes the exam.

It doesn't matter how long they will have dated before they get married.

Future Perfect Tense

CONDITIONS AND CONSEQUENCES

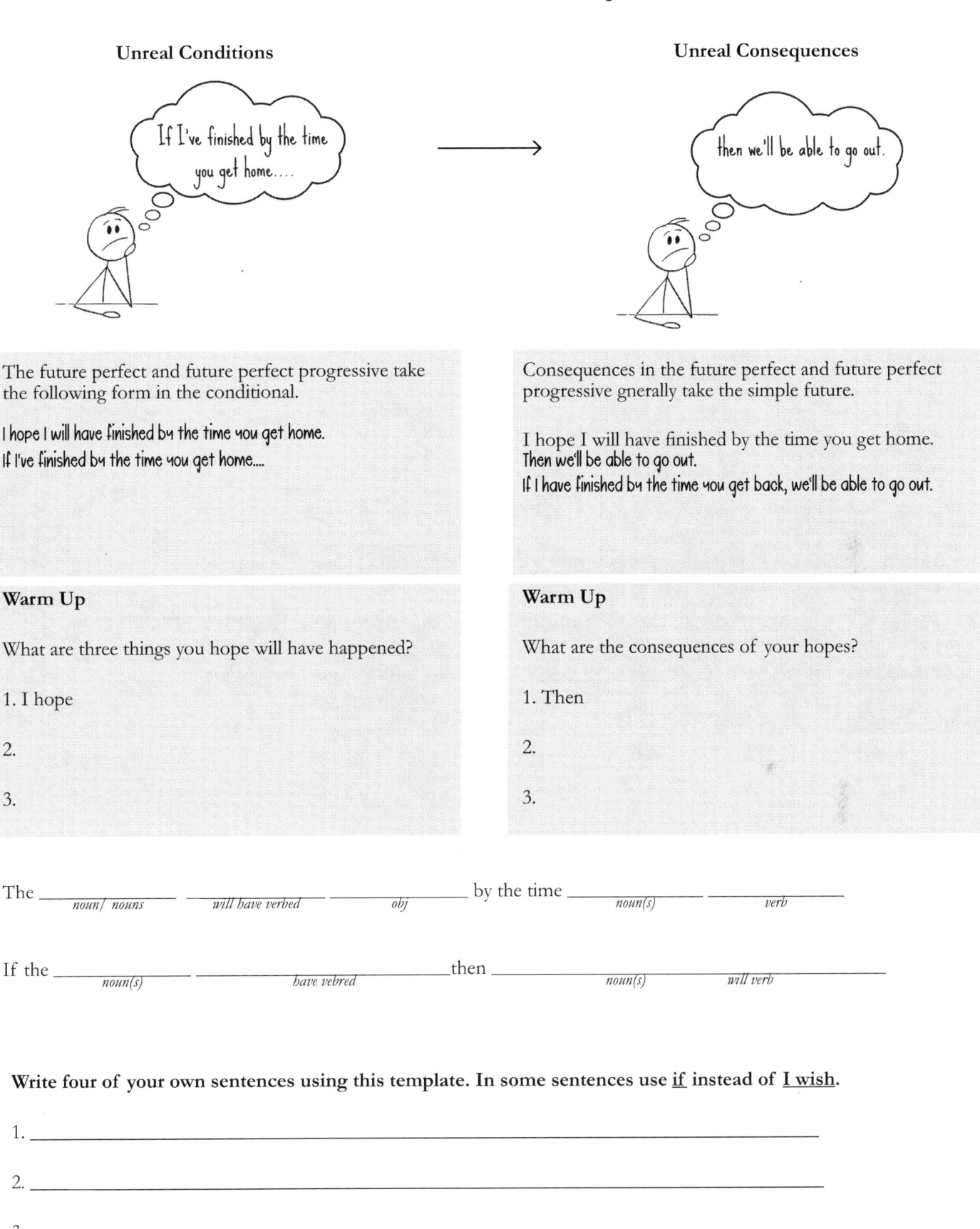

Unreal Conditions

If I've finished by the time you get home....

→

Unreal Consequences

then we'll be able to go out.

The future perfect and future perfect progressive take the following form in the conditional.

I hope I will have finished by the time you get home.
If I've finished by the time you get home....

Consequences in the future perfect and future perfect progressive gnerally take the simple future.

I hope I will have finished by the time you get home.
Then we'll be able to go out.
If I have finished by the time you get back, we'll be able to go out.

Warm Up

What are three things you hope will have happened?

1. I hope

2.

3.

Warm Up

What are the consequences of your hopes?

1. Then

2.

3.

The _____ _____ _____ by the time _____ _____
     noun/ nouns   *will have verbed*   *obj*   *noun(s)*   *verb*

If the _____ _____then _____ _____
      noun(s)   *have vebred*   *noun(s)*   *will verb*

Write four of your own sentences using this template. In some sentences use <u>if</u> instead of <u>I wish</u>.

1. _____

2. _____

3. _____

4. _____

Future Perfect Tense

PRACTICAL APPLICATION

Read the following short paragraph. <u>Underline</u> the verbs in future perfect tense.

A Big Life Change

By the time I go back home, I <u>will have had</u> some great experiences here in the States. I <u>will have gone</u> **celebrity hunting** in Hollywood. I <u>will have gone</u> snowboarding in the Rocky Mountains. I <u>will have gone</u> **snorkeling** in the Gulf of Mexico, **parasailing** off the coast of the Atlantic, and **bungee jumping** from Niagara Falls. But my trip <u>won't have been</u> all play. Since I'm studying at a language institute right now, I hope that I <u>will have made</u> some progress learning English. Every morning, I get up and **cram** for four solid hours. My grammar book is super **wrinkled** and **dog-eared**. My old fashioned **hardback** dictionary is practically **torn to shreds**. I think my teachers are **bleary-eyed** and **exasperated** from all the emails I send them. But it's worth it. By the time I get on the plane and head for home, I <u>will have been speaking</u> English daily for six whole months. Surely that <u>will have made</u> a positive impact on my language skills.

NOTES: Use this space to write notes about the usage of this tense.

---

celebrity hunting: searching for celebrities

snorkeling: swimming in the sea

parasailing: flying behind a ship with a parachute

bungee jumping: jumping from high up with a cord

cram: study hard

wrinkled: creased

dog-eared: with wrinkled edges

hardback: book with hard cover

torn to shreds: ripped up

bleary-eyed: red eyed

exasperated: overwhelmed

Future Perfect Tense

Now you try! Write a paragraph in which you describe things you <u>will have accomplished</u> or by a date in the future.

Future Perfect Tense

SENTENCES IN FUTURE PERFECT TENSE

LEVEL I

The dolphin will have swum home by tomorrow.
_____ will have _____ by _____ .
   NP   *VP+past participle*   *time word*

LEVEL II

The dolphin will have swum home by the time the sun sets tomorrow.
_____ will have _____ by the time _____ .
   NP   *VP+past participle*   *clause+present tense*

LEVEL III

The dolphin will have swum home and gone to bed by the time the sun sets tomorrow.
_____ will have _____ and _____ by the time _____ .
   NP   *VP+past participle*   *VP+past particple*   *clause+present tense*

Note: Practice Pages utilize the generative rules introduced in the introduction to students section to encourage students to make as creative sentences as possible.

Simple Sentence
S → NP VP

Verb Phrase:
VP → (Adv) V (NP) (NP) (PP) (Adv)
VP → (Adv) V (VP) (PP) (Adv)

Noun Phrase:
NP → (Art) (Adj*) N (RC) (PP)

Adv = Adverb: *always, often, quickly, suddenly*
PP = Prepositional Phrase: *in, on, from*
Art = Article: *a, an, the*
Adj = Adjectives: *cute, fluffy, white*
RC = Relative Clause: the cat *that I saw at the shelter*

Parentheses () means optional
Asterick * means can have multiple

Future Perfect Tense

PRACTICE SENTENCES

1. _____
   _____
2. _____
   _____
3. _____
   _____

1. _____
   _____
2. _____
   _____
3. _____
   _____

1. _____
   _____
2. _____
   _____
3. _____
   _____

Notes: Use this space to note common mistakes, instances you can use the tense or anything that helps you use the tense.

Future Perfect Tense

QUESTIONS IN FUTURE PERFECT TENSE

LEVEL I

(Where)   will   the dolphin have   swum   by   tomorrow?
(_____) will _____ have _____ by _____ ?
  Wh-word   *NP*   *VP+Past Participle*   *time*

LEVEL II

(Where)   will   the dolphin have   swum   by the time   the sun sets tomorrow?
(_____) will _____ have _____ by the time _____ ?
  Wh-word   *NP*   *VP+Past Participle*   *clause+present tense*

LEVEL III

(Where)   will   the dolphin have   swum   and   gone to bed   by   the time sun sets tomorrow?
(_____) will _____ have _____ and _____ by _____ ?
  Wh-word   *NP*   *VP+Past Participle*   *VP+Past Participle*   *clause+present tense*

Note: Practice Pages utilize the generative rules introduced in the introduction to students section to encourage students to make as creative sentences as possible.

Simple Sentence
S → NP VP

Verb Phrase:
VP → (Adv) V (NP) (NP) (PP) (Adv)
VP → (Adv) V (VP) (PP) (Adv)

Noun Phrase:
NP → (Art) (Adj*) N (RC) (PP)

Adv = Adverb: *always, often, quickly, suddenly*
PP = Prepositional Phrase: *in, on, from*
Art = Article: *a, an, the*
Adj = Adjectives: *cute, fluffy, white*
RC = Relative Clause: the cat *that I saw at the shelter*

Parentheses () means optional
Asterick * means can have multiple

Future Perfect Tense

PRACTICE SENTENCES

1. _____
   _____
2. _____
   _____
3. _____
   _____

1. _____
   _____
2. _____
   _____
3. _____
   _____

1. _____
   _____
2. _____
   _____
3. _____
   _____

Notes: Use this space to note common mistakes, instances you can use the tense or anything that helps you use the tense.

Future Perfect Tense

NEGATIVE STATEMENTS IN FUTURE PERFECT TENSE

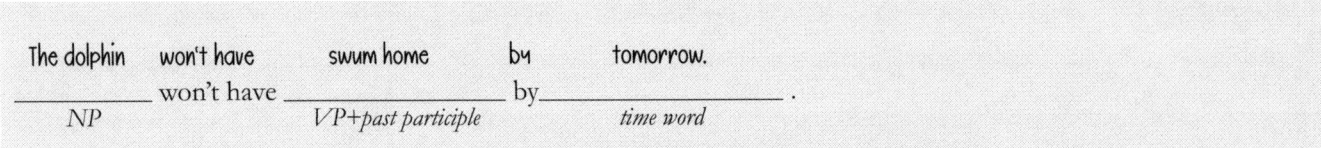

LEVEL I

The dolphin   won't have   swum home   by   tomorrow.
_____ won't have _____ by _____ .
   NP   VP+past participle   time word

LEVEL II

The dolphin   won't have   swum home   by the time   the sun sets tomorrow.
_____ won't have _____ by the time _____ .
   NP   VP+past participle   clause+present tense

LEVEL III

The dolphin   won't have   swum home   and   gone to bed   by the time   the sun sets tomorrow.
_____ won't have _____ and _____ by the time _____ .
   NP   VP+past participle   VP+past participle   clause+present tense

Note: Practice Pages utilize the generative rules introduced in the introduction to students section to encourage students to make as creative sentences as possible.

Simple Sentence
S → NP VP

Verb Phrase:
VP → (Adv) V (NP) (NP) (PP) (Adv)
VP → (Adv) V (VP) (PP) (Adv)

Noun Phrase:
NP → (Art) (Adj*) N (RC) (PP)

Adv = Adverb: *always, often, quickly, suddenly*
PP = Prepositional Phrase: *in, on, from*
Art = Article: *a, an, the*
Adj = Adjectives: *cute, fluffy, white*
RC = Relative Clause: the cat *that I saw at the shelter*

Parentheses () means optional
Asterick * means can have multiple

Future Perfect Tense

PRACTICE SENTENCES

1. _____
2. _____
3. _____

1. _____
2. _____
3. _____

1. _____
2. _____
3. _____

Notes: Use this space to note common mistakes, instances you can use the tense or anything that helps you use the tense.

Future Perfect Tense

NOUN CLAUSES IN FUTURE PERFECT TENSE

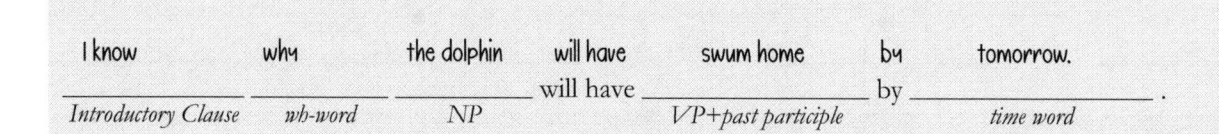

LEVEL I

I know _____ why _____ the dolphin _____ will have _____ swum home _____ by _____ tomorrow _____.
Introductory Clause — *wh-word* — *NP* — *VP+past participle* — *time word*

LEVEL II

I know _____ why _____ the dolphin _____ will have _____ swum home _____ by the time _____ the sun sets _____.
Introductory Clause — *wh-word* — *NP* — *VP+past participle* — *clause+present tense*

LEVEL III

I know _____ why _____ the dolphin _____ will have _____ swum home _____ and _____ gone to bed _____ by the time _____ the sun sets _____.
Introductory Clause — *wh-word* — *NP* — *VP+past participle* — *VP+past participle* — *clause+present tense*

Note: Practice Pages utilize the generative rules introduced in the introduction to students section to encourage students to make as creative sentences as possible.

Simple Sentence
S → NP VP

Verb Phrase:
VP → (Adv) V (NP) (NP) (PP) (Adv)
VP → (Adv) V (VP) (PP) (Adv)

Noun Phrase:
NP → (Art) (Adj*) N (RC) (PP)

Adv = Adverb: *always, often, quickly, suddenly*
PP = Prepositional Phrase: *in, on, from*
Art = Article: *a, an, the*
Adj = Adjectives: *cute, fluffy, white*
RC = Relative Clause: *the cat that I saw at the shelter*

Parentheses () means optional
Asterick * means can have multiple

Future Perfect Tense

PRACTICE SENTENCES

1. _____
_____
2. _____
_____
3. _____
_____

1. _____
_____
2. _____
_____
3. _____
_____

1. _____
_____
2. _____
_____
3. _____
_____

Notes: Use this space to note common mistakes, instances you can use the tense or anything that helps you use the tense.

ADJECTIVE CLAUSES

The person
- Who verbs
- Who noun verbs ("who" can be omitted)
- Whose noun verbs
- Whose noun noun verbs
- Whom noun verbs prep ("whom" can be omitted)

The thing
- which verbs / that
- (which) noun verbs / (that) noun verbs

The place → where noun verbs

The time → when noun verbs

The reason → why noun verbs

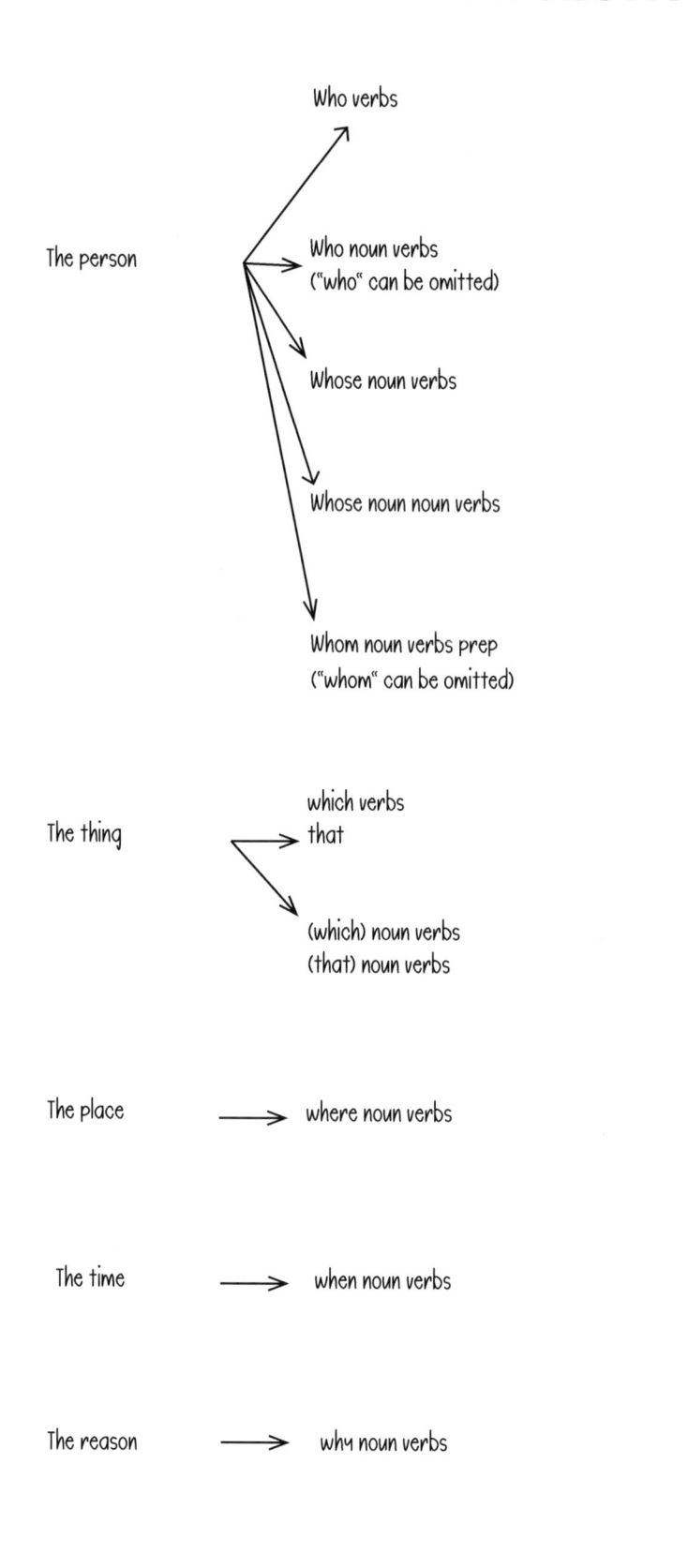

The man who teaches...
The man who teaches eats apples.
I know the man who teaches.

The man who the cat scratched...
The man who the cat scratched eats apples.
I know the man who the cat scratched.

The man whose car goes fast...
The man whose car goes fast eats apples.
I know the man whose car goes fast.

The man whose car I borrowed..
The man whose car I borrowed eats apples.
I know the man whose car I borrowed.

The man whom I gave the letter to...
The man whom I gave the letter to eats apples.
I know the man whom I gave the letter to.

The car that goes fast...
The car that goes fast needs gas.
I borrowed the car that goes fast.

The car that the man borrowed...
The car that the man borrowed is blue.
I know the car that the man borrowed.

The country where my father lives
The country where my father lives has hills.
I know the country where my father lives.

The day when I left...
The day when I left was cold.
I know the day when I left.

The reason why I love you...
The reason why I love you is complex.
I know the reason why I love you.

Adjective Clauses

Now you Practice!

For each adjective clause type write one base adjective clause and two sentences.

The person who verbs (The man who teaches)	Adjective Clause <u>the man who teaches</u> 1. <u>The man who teaches eats apples</u> 2. _____
The person who noun verbs (The man who the cat scratched)	Adjective Clause _____ 1. _____ 2. _____
The person whose noun noun verbs (The man whose car I borrowed)	Adjective Clause _____ 1. _____ 2. _____
Ther person whom noun verbs prep (The man whom I gave the letter to)	Adjective Clause _____ 1. _____ 2. _____
The thing which/that verbs (The car that goes fast)	Adjective Clause _____ 1. _____ 2. _____
The thing which/that noun verbs (The car that the man borrowed)	Adjective Clause _____ 1. _____ 2. _____
The place where verbs (The country where my father lives)	Adjective Clause _____ 1. _____ 2. _____
The time when noun verbs (The day when I left)	Adjective Clause _____ 1. _____ 2. _____

BASIC TIME CLAUSES

Time Word	Past	Present	Future
While	When the sun **shone**, the snow **melted**.	When the sun **shines**, the snow **melts**.	When the sun **shines**, the snow **will melt**.
Whenever	Whenever the rain **fell**, the grass **grew**.	Whenever the rain **fell**, the grass **grew**.	Whenever the rain **falls**, the grass **will grow**.
Before	Before I **ate**, I **cooked**.	Before I **eat**, I **cook**.	Before I **eat**, I'll **cook**.
After	After I **cooked**, I **ate**.	After I **cook**, I **eat**.	After I **cook**, I'll **eat**.
As Soon As	As soon as the alarm **rang**, I **woke** up.	As soon as the alarm **rings**, I **wake** up.	As soon as the alarm **rings**, I'll **wake** up.
While	While you **slept**, I **worked**.	While you **sleep**, I **work**.	While **you** **sleep**, I'll **work**.
While Progressive	While you **were sleeping**, I **was working**.	While you're **sleeping**, I'm **working**.	While you are **sleeping**, I'll **be working**.

Basic Time Clauses

Now You Practice!

For each time clause type write one base adverb clause and two sentences

When

When the sun shines, the ice melts.

Time Clause <u>When I called home yesterday</u>

1. <u>When I called home yesterday, my mother told me a story.</u>

2. _____

Whenever

Whenever the rain falls, the grass grows.

Adjective Clause <u>Whenever</u>

1. _____

2. _____

Before

Before I eat, I cook.

Adjective Clause <u>Before</u>

1. _____

2. _____

After

After I cook, I eat.

Adjective Clause <u>After</u>

1. _____

2. _____

As Soon As

As soon as the alarm rings, I wake up.

Adjective Clause <u>As soon as</u>

1. _____

2. _____

While

Since *while* allows for more complex sentences try to do four with while.

While you slept, I was working.

While you're sleeping I'm working.

While you sleep, I'll be working.

Adjective Clause <u>While</u>

1. _____

2. _____

3. _____

4. _____

TYPES OF FREQUENCY

Adverb	Freq	B	M	E	Write an Example Sentence
Always	100%		√		
Almost always	99%		√		
Often	50-75%		√		
Sometimes	25-50%	√	√	√	
Rarely	10-25%		√		
Every now and again	10-15%	√		√	
Almost never	1%		√		
Never	0%		√		
Every Second		√		√	
Every hour		√		√	
Every day		√		√	
Every Monday		√		√	
Twice a week				√	
Three times a year				√	
Annually				√	

Sentence Placement: B / M / E

HOW OFTEN DO YOU...?

> Eat vegetables, breathe, call your mother, write a poem, go to the gym, smoke cigarettes, practice drawing, wake up at night, dream, think about your job, think about money, think about love, worry, drink alcohol, go dancing, buy new shoes, buy gas, drive over the speed limit, eat junk food, sing in the shower

Talk to your classmates. Find out how often they do certain things. Answer with a because.

Jeremy, how often do you exercise? I never exercise because I am perfect.

1.

2.

3.

4.

5.

Types of Frequency

PRACTICE WITH WHEN, WHENEVER & EVERY TIME

> When, whenever, and every time also allow us to talk about frequency. In general these adverbials link two clauses together to show that when A happens, B also happens.

Examples:

Every time it rains, I get my umbrella.

When it rains, I get my umbrella.

Whenever it rains, I get my umbrella.

Fill in the blanks.

Whenever the sun rises, _____

Every time it snows, _____

Whenever I see my spouse, _____

When my mother texts me, _____

Every time my phone buzzes, _____

Whenever I study English, _____

When the light turns yellow, _____

When the alarm goes off, _____

Whenever I check the news, _____

Now, write three of your own examples:

1. _____

2. _____

3. _____

Types of Frequency

Now You Practice!

> "Only when" suggests that certain things happen at one time and at no other. A **only happens when B happens.**

Examples

I love netflix, but I **only** watch shows **when** I'm not busy.

I'm not a vegetarian, but I only eat meat when I'm very hungry.

I sometimes play chess, but I **only** play video games when I'm bored.

Now you practice:

Tell me how your habits are different in different situations using "when"

Although I usually _____ when it's summer, I only _____ when winter comes.

Although I often _____ when it's morning, I only _____ when it's late at night.

Although I usually _____ when I'm with my friends, I only _____ when I'm with my family.

Although I usually _____ when I'm tired, I only _____ when I feel energetic.

Now, write three of your own examples:

1. _____

2. _____

3. _____

Facts and Stative Verbs

The simple present is also used in two other circumstances: to describe

* Facts
* Stative verbs

For now, we will call a fact, a statement which we believe is frequently true about the world. For example, the sky might not be blue right now, but it's blue every day. So, we consider this to be a fact.

The sky is blue. Birds fly. Cats meow. The capital of Colombia is Bogota. In the space below, brainstorm some facts about nature, people, America, and things. Let's see what we can come up with as a class.

Nature	People	America	Things
The ocean is salty.	Vanessa is my little sister.	Texas is hot.	Violins make really-beautiful music.

Facts and Stative Verbs

EMOTIONS	BELIEFS	OWNING	SENSES	SEEMING
like	think	have	see	seem
love	know	own	taste	appear
hate	remember	possess	hear	look like
need	suppose	belong	smell	resemble
want	guess	owe	know	
fear	imagine		sound	
envy	feel			
mind	understand			

In general, these verbs do not take -ing.

For example: I own a car. NOT I am owning a car.

Write five of your own sentences using stative verbs:

1. _____

2. _____

3. _____

4. _____

5. _____

PROBABILITY AND CERTAINTY (POSITIVE)

50% certainty
(could, might, may, all possible)

50% certainty
(could, might, may, all possible)

Past	I don't see the mouse. The cat <u>could have eaten</u> it.	I don't see the mouse. The cat <u>must have eaten</u> the mouse.
Past Continous	What was the cat doing yesterday? She <u>could have been</u> <u>eating</u> the mouse.	What was the cat doing yesterday? She <u>had to have been eating</u> the mouse.
Present	Where is the mouse? She <u>could be</u> inside the cat's stomach.	Where is the mouse? She <u>has to be</u> inside the cat's stomach.
Present Continous	Where is the cat? She <u>could be eating</u> the mouse.	Where is the cat? She <u>must be eating</u> the mouse.
Future	What will the cat do tomorrow? She <u>might eat</u> the mouse.	What will the cat do tomorrow? She's <u>probably going to eat</u>* the mouse. ("should eat" is also possible)
Future Continous	What will the cat <u>be doing</u> tomorrow? She <u>might be eating</u> the mouse.	What will the cat <u>be doing</u> tomorrow? She's <u>probably going to be eating</u> the mouse. ("should be eating" is also possible)

Now You Practice!

Circle the correct answer:

1. Sorry! I don't know anyone with that name.
You *should have/ must have* the wrong number.

2. Where's Saeed? He's not under the table!
I don't know. He *might be/ should be* at home.

3. This jacket is too small for me, but it *might fit/ should fit/ must fit* Sofien.

4. The students are yawning.
They *might be/ should be/ must be* bored.

5. Andrea is shivering.
She *might be/ should be/ must be* cold.

6. The doorbell rang. But I didn't answer it because I was sleeping.
I guess it *might have been/ should have been/ must have been* my neighbor.

7. Busra didn't come to class on Monday.
She *might have been/ should have been/ must have been* afraid of the thunder.

8. I saw Saeed with a woman!
It *might be/ should be/ must be* his wife.

9. She is carrying a wet umbrella.
It *might be raining/ should be raining/ must be raining* outside.

10. Do you smell smoke?
Something *might be burnng/ should be burning/ must be burning*.

11. It's really noisy upstairs.
The children *might be playing/ should be playing/ must be playing* a game.

Probability and Certainty (Negative)

50% certainty
(might not or may not)

100% certainty
(must not, couldn't, can't)

Past	I thought the cat ate the mouse. But I heard a squeak. I guess the cat <u>might not have eaten</u> it.	I don't see the mouse. But the cat was sleeping. She <u>couldn't have eaten</u> it!
Past Continous	I saw the cat eating yesterday, but I don't know. She <u>might not have been eating</u> the mouse.	What was the cat doing yesterday? I don't know. But I just saw a mouse. She <u>couldn't have been eating</u> it.
Present	I don't see the cat. She <u>might not be</u> here.	Where is the mouse? I just heard a squeak. She <u>must not be</u> inside the cat's stomach.
Present Continous	The cat likes to sleep, but she <u>might not be sleeping</u> now.	I just heard a squeak. It's the mouse again. The cat <u>must not be eating</u> it.
Future	The cat sees the mouse. But <u>she might not eat</u> it.	What will the cat do tomorrow? She's <u>probably not going to eat</u>* the mouse.
Future Continous	(Rarely used)	What will the cat <u>be doing</u> tomorrow? She's proba-bly <u>not going to be eating</u> the mouse. ("should be eating" is also possible)

198

Probability and Certainty (Negative)

Now You Practice!

Circle the correct answer:

1. 2+2 doesn't equal 5! Your calculations *can't be/might not be/should not be* right!

2. Andrae didn't eat the snack! She *can't be/might not be/should not be* hungry.

3. Sofien said he didn't go out last weekend. But that *can't be/might not be/should not be* true.

4. What's that noise? It *can't be/might not be/should not be* a dog. It's coming from the sky! Dogs don't fly.

5. What's that? It *can't be/might not be/should not be* a dragon. Dragons don't exist!

6. Louisa didn't come to class on Monday. She *can't feel like/might not feel like/should not feel like* driving.

7. Louisa came to class on Monday and looked great. She *can't be/might not be/should not be* sick.

8. Andrea seemed very cheerful this morning. She *can't have stayed up/might not have stayed up/should not have stayed up* late last night.

9. Busra's hair looks the same. She *can't have gotten/might not have gotten/should not have gotten* it cut.

10. You're bone dry. It *can't be raining/might not be raining/nust not be raining* outside.

11. The ground is dry. It *can't have rained/might not have rained/nust not have rained* last night.

12. It's really quiet upstairs. The children *can't be playing/might not be playing/should not be playing* their game anymore.

THE THREE CANS

	Abilty	Opportunity	Permission
Present	I can speak English	I can travel to Europe!	I can stay home on Monday.
Past	I could speak English before, but I can't now.	I could have traveled to Europe last year.	I was allowed to stay home on Monday.
Future	Next year, I will be able to speak English.	Next year, I'll have the chance to go to Europe.	I'll be allowed to stay home on Monday.
Present Unreal Conditional	If I lived in America, I would be able to speak English.	If I had money I would have the chance to go to Europe.	If I had a better job, I would be allowed to stay home on Monday.
Past Unreal Conditional	If I had grown up in America, then I would have been able to speak English	If I had had the money last year, I would have had the chance to go to Europe.	If I had called my boss, I would have been allowed to stay home on Monday.

Brainstorm!

What you can you do now?

when you were a child?

in the future?

Are these abilities, opportunities or permissions?

Now You Practice!
Tell me about your abilities, opportunities, and permissions

When I was a child....

Now...

Next year...

Coulda, Shoulda, Woulda, Will

	Opportunity	Advisability	Result
Present	I guess I <u>could study</u> English	In fact, maybe I *<u>should</u>* study English.	Then I<u>'ll be able to</u> speak English.
Past	I guess I <u>could have</u> studied English.	In fact, maybe I <u>should have</u> studied English!	Then I <u>would speak</u> English now. or Then I <u>would have learned</u> English.
Future	I <u>can study</u> English next semester.	I <u>should</u> study English next semester.	Then I<u>'ll learn</u> how to speak English

Brainstorm!
In the space below tell me about some opportunities that you have now and some opportunies you had in the past. Should you do those things? Should you have done them? What results would ensue?

Coulda, Shoulda, Woulda, Will

GET TO VS. HAVE TO

☺ ☹

Present	Yay! I <u>get to</u> go to the zoo!	Boo! I <u>have to</u> work! or I <u>got to</u> work!
Past	Yay! I <u>got to</u> the zoo last weekend.	Boo! I <u>had to</u> work!
Future	Yay! I'm <u>going to get to go</u> to the zoo this weekend.	Boo! I'm <u>going to have to</u> work!
Present Unreal	If I <u>had</u> the time, I <u>would get to</u> go to the zoo!	If it <u>were</u> Monday, then I <u>would have to</u> work.
Past Unreal	If I <u>had had</u> time, I <u>would have gotten to</u> got to the zoo.	If it <u>had been</u> Monday, I <u>would have had to</u> work.

Brainstorm!
In the space below tell me about some things you had to do and some things you got to do last weekend. If things <u>had been different</u> would you <u>not have gotten to</u> do those things?

PRACTICAL APPLICATION

Read the following short paragraph. <u>Underline</u> the modals. (Circle) the conditionals.

Regrets, Regrets, Regrets..

I have to admit that I don't have very many talents. I wish I could sing. But, frankly, I can't. My wife says that, at church, when we sing hymns, I sound like a **rusty spigot**. I just **croak** and **sputter**. Oh well. I just never learned. I wish I had practiced more. Then maybe I would have even learned how to play an instrument. And I definitely would be able to **carry a tune**. Another talent I lack is the ability to play sports. I run like I have **lead** feet. I just **plod** and **totter**. I guess I just wasn't interested when I was younger. But I wish I had been more athletic. Then maybe I wouldn't feel so out of shape now. Finally, I really don't have a **lick** of fashion sense. I can't coordinate colors. I can't match. I can't tell you what goes with what. I guess I just never had much **aptitute** or curiosity about fashion. I wish I had been able to learn more about it thought. It would have been nice to be a **spiffy** dresser when I was younger. Although there are a lot of things I can't do, I'm proud of what I can do. For example, I'm a great student. Although my English isn't perfect, I study every day. I'm sure that, by this time next year, I'll be able to speak fluently.

NOTES:

---

rusty: covered with rust

spigot: faucet

croak: frog sound

sputter: stammer.

carry a tune: sustain a rhythm

lead feet: feet made of metal

plod: run slowly

a lick of: a small amount of

aptitude: talent

spiffy: fashionable

Now You Practice!

Write a paragraph in which you tell me about some regrets that you have...

TALKING ABOUT DURATION....

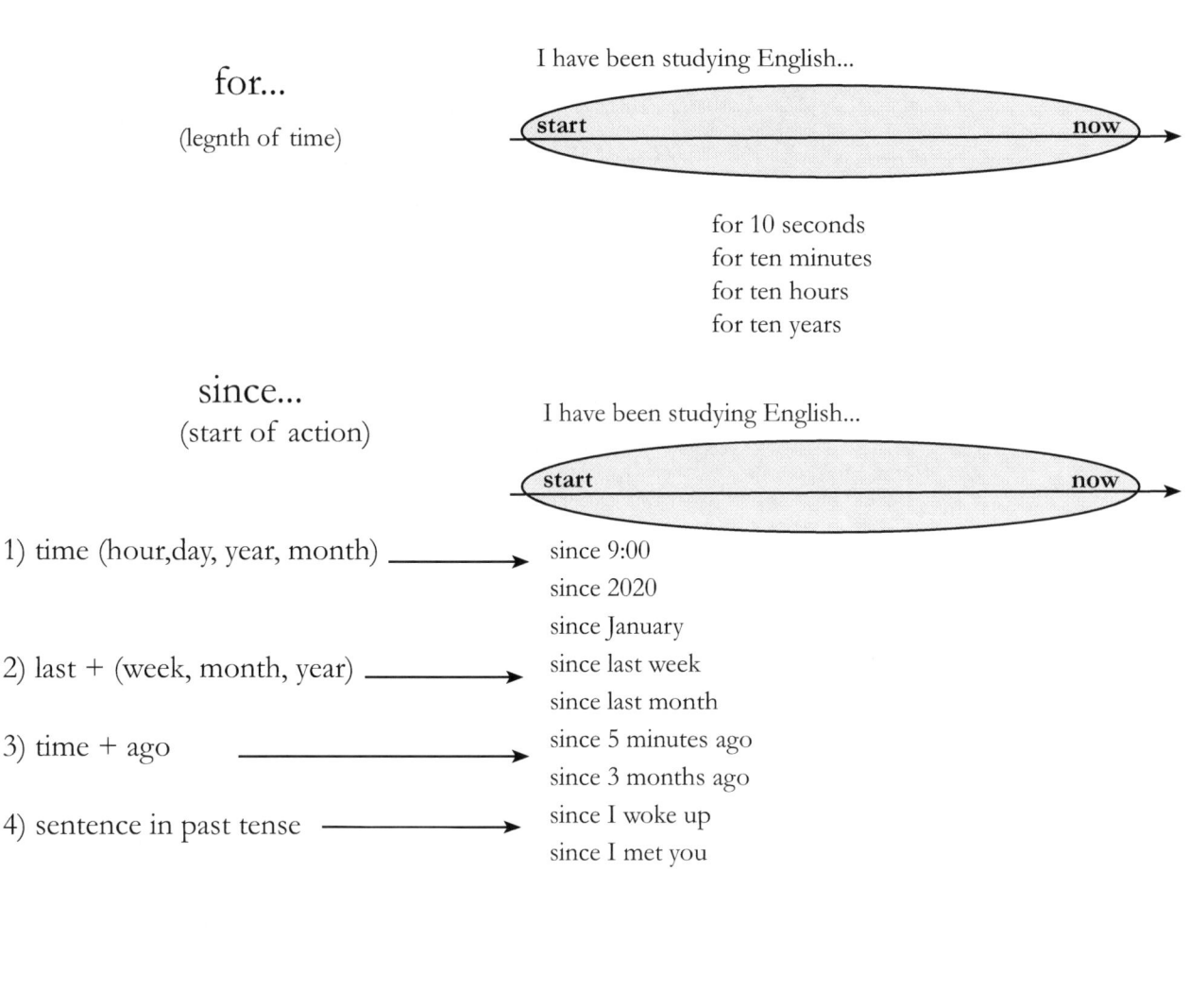

for...
(legnth of time)

I have been studying English...

start — now

for 10 seconds
for ten minutes
for ten hours
for ten years

since...
(start of action)

I have been studying English...

start — now

1) time (hour, day, year, month) → since 9:00
since 2020
since January

2) last + (week, month, year) → since last week
since last month

3) time + ago → since 5 minutes ago
since 3 months ago

4) sentence in past tense → since I woke up
since I met you

for as long as...
(duration of 2nd action)

I have been studying English...

start — now

* the second sentence must be either in the present perfect or present perfect progressive

for as long as <u>the sun has been shining</u>.

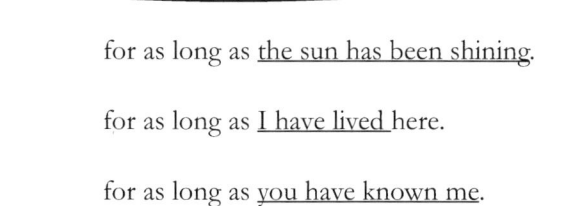

for as long as <u>I have lived</u> here.

for as long as <u>you have known me</u>.

-ING OR NOT?

Situations OR Stative Verbs	Actions
I have known you for years.	I have been sleeping for hours.
I have worked here for years.	I have been studying for hours.
I have lived here for years.	I have been shopping for hours.
I have felt happy for years.	I have been partying for hours.
Other examples?	Other examples?

Certain activities can be EITHER actions or situations depending on the context. For example: working, playing music, running, swimming, etc.

Emphasizes that this something the speaker does habitually.

Emphasizes that this is a recent, continuing action.

I have played violin for years.

I have been playing violin for an hour.

PRESENT, PAST, AND FUTURE...
I HAVE BEEN STUDYING ENGLISH...

present
(actions which started in the past and have been continuing until now)

start ——————— now

for an hour.

since 9:00

since 10 minutes ago.

for as long as the sun had beeb shining.

past
(actions which started in the past and continued until an *interruption*)

1) time (hour, day, year, month)

2) last + (week, month, year)

3) time + ago

4) sentence in past tense

I **had been studying** English...

start ——————— end   now

* for two hours when <u>the phone rang</u>.

* since 9:00 when <u>the phone rang</u>.

* since 10 minutes ago when <u>the phone rang</u>.

* for as long as the sun had been shining when <u>the phone rang</u>.

I **will have been studying** English...

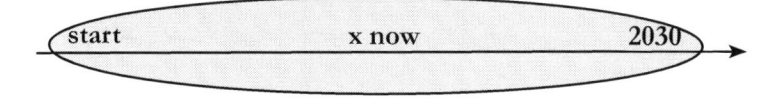

start ——————— x now ——————— 2030

for 10 years **by 2030**

for 10 years **by the time I leave America.**

future
(duration of action that will be ongoing in the future.

* by TIME
(by 2030)

* by the time that NOUN VERBS
(by the time I <u>get</u> home).

Now You Practice!

Write sentences in present past and future using the following verbs.

Andrea / study medicine/ ten minutes.

Present:

Past:

Future:

Saeed/ dance/ half-an-hour

Present:

Past:

Future:

Abeer/ cook/ three hours

Present:

Past:

Future:

Present, Past, and Future...

Quick Practice...

I _____ soccer for three years. How long _____ soccer?
(play) (you, play)

Tom: Oh, you live in Rio! How long _____ here?
(be)

Sue: We _____ here for three years.
(be)

I _____ the same phone for two years. I want a new one.
(have)

I _____ basketball since I was a child. I play all the time.
(love)

Frank _____ for McDonalds since he graduated from Harvard University.
(work)

I _____ James for three years, and I _____ changes in his life.
(know) (notice)

Do you love me? Yes I _____ you
(love)

ever since I _____ my eyes on you.
(lay)

How long _____?
(she study)

She _____
(study)

for as long as she _____ in that desk.
(sit)

Do You... How Long Have You...

Ask your classmates....

Talk to your classmates about their hobbies and interests. Try to find out how long they have been doing certain things.

Do you play an instrument?

Yes, I play the piano.

How long have you been playing the piano?

I've been playing the piano for 2 years.

---

be awake, breathe, study English, play musical instrument, play sport, live in current location, work current job, be married, be single, know best friend, participate in a hobby

GERUNDS VS INFINITIVES: THE BASICS

GERUNDS (VERBING)

1) Can be used <u>either</u> at the begining or end of a sentence.

Dancing is fun.
I like dancing.

In this case, gerunds are used like nouns.

2) Often follow prepositions.

Tell me <u>about</u> dancing.
I have heard <u>of</u> dancing.

3) Often follow "go"

Let's <u>go</u> dancing.

4) Can follow possessives

I've seen <u>his</u> dancing.

5) Commonly follow certain verbs. (with or without an object).

He <u>imagined</u> dancing.
He imagined <u>his wife</u> dancings.

6) Occur as a part of special expressions.

They <u>had fun</u> dancing.

INFINITIVES (TO VERB)

1) Can be used either at the beginning or end of a sentence though <u>much</u> more common at the end.

I like to dance.

2) Can occur after certain adjectives.

He is <u>happy</u> to dance.

3) Commonly follow certain verbs (with or without an object)

He <u>expected</u> to dance.
He expected <u>his wife</u> to dance.

4) Commonly follow certain nouns

He had a <u>chance</u> to dance.

USING GERUNDS AFTER PREPOSITIONS

(most common examples)

	to	of	about	for	in	with	from
Noun + Preposition	addiction to reaction to	advantage of fear of habit of knowledge of love of	anxiety about story about	credit for responsibility for	belief in experience in interest in		
Adjective + Preposition	dedicated to used to	afraid of capable of *tired of *bored of * (felt **during** the activity)	happy about sad about worried about	responsible for	interested in involved in	dissapointed with happy with	*tired from (bored from) * (felt **after** the activity)
Verb + Preposition			care about talk about explain about complain about tell about argue about	don't care for	succeed in believe in involve in	agree with	

213

Using Gerunds After Prepositions

Now you practice!
(add the preposition and verb below)

His reaction _____ the race showed poor sportsmanship.
      (lose)

She has a habit _____ very loudly.
      (laugh)

Luckily, we don't have much anxiety_____ to a new city.
          (move)

My boss always wants to take credit _____ the work that I did!
         (do)

Athletes have to be dedicated _____ all season.
        (train)

I live right next to the night club, so I'm used _____ that awful disco music.
         (hear)

Why do you look so beat? I'm tired _____.
        (exercise)

Let's stop now. I'm tired _____.
      (exercise)

I think we should talk_____ English better.
      (study)

She's a health-nut. She really believes _____ right every day.
        (eat)

This appartment isn't very good. I'm dissapointed _____ here.
        (live)

Using Gerunds After Prepositions

INFITIVE OR GERUND AFTER VERBS
(most common examples)

Verbs followed by gerunds	Verbs followed by infinitives	Verbs followed by either (no difference in meaning)
admit	agree	
advise	appear	can't stand
allow	arrange	continue
anticipate	ask	hate
appreciate	don't care	like
avoid	choose claim	love
can't help	continue	neglect
can't see	decide	prefer
complete	demand	propose
consider	deserve	
defend	expect	
delay	fail	
deny	hesitate	
despise	hope	
discuss	intend	
dislike	learn	
don't mind	manage	
encourage	need	
enjoy	offer	
finish	plan	
imagine	prefer	
involve	prepare	
keep	pretend	
mention	promise	
miss	refuse	
postpone	seem	
practice	swear	
recall	tend	
report	wait	
resist	want	
risk		
suggest		
understand		

Using Gerunds After Prepositions

Now you practice!
(add the preposition and verb below)

I can't stand_____ in traffic when I'm in a hurry.
     (wait)

She is learning _____ the violin with her women's group.
    (play)

Although he had failed many times, he kept_____ to learn English grammar..
                (try)

I am an introvert, so I dislike_____ to nightclubs.!
         (go)

I got a C on the exam. I really need _____more diligently.
           (study)

I have never been to Colombia, but I plan _____ soon.
           (go)

I don't mind _____ a little extra for good service.
    (pay)

Although the student deny _____, the professor was suspicious.
        (cheat)

I think we should talk_____ English better.
      (study)

I can't help_____ when I hear something funny.
    (chuckle)

Can you believe he claims _____ six feet tall?.
      (be)

A Few Tricky Words

(These words take <u>either</u> gerund or infinitve with a slight difference in meaning)

Main Verb	+ to V	+ving
Remember	"Remember to verb" is used to talk about a task. I remembered to do my homework.	"Remember verbing" is used to talk about a memory. I remember seeing the cute dog.
Forget	"Forget to verb" is used to talk about a task. I forgot to do my homework.	"Forget verbing" is used to talk about a memory. I forgot seeing the cute dog.
Keep	"Keep noun to verb" is used to describe the purpose of a thing. I keep a dog to protect my house.	"Keep verbing" is used to describe a continuing action. When I'm happy, I keep talking and talking.
Need	"Need to verb" is used for a person. The woman needs to wash her car.	"Need verbing" is used for a thing. That car needs washing.
Start	"Start to verb" is used when "start" is in a continous tense. He is starting to learn English.	"Start verbing" is used in non-progressive tenses. He started learning English.
Stop	"Stop to verb" is used to mean "stop in order to." She stopped to drink, because she was thirsty.	"Stop verbing" means to quit She stopped drinking, because alcohol is unhealthy.
Try	"Try to verb" means to attempt and fail. He tried to climb the tree, but it was too high.	"Try verbing" means to try something as an experiment. She tried eating vegan for a month, but she missed bacon too much.

A Few Tricky Words

Now you practice!
(add the preposition and verb below)

Oh no! I forgot _____ my rent this month!
                (pay)

Thankfully, I remembered _____ my landlord and apologize.
                        (call)

Have we met before. I forget_____ you.
                              (meet)

I remember _____ that song. What a catchy tune!
                      (hear)

I keep a juice box in my pocket_____ if I get thirsty.
                                  (drink)

How frustrating! I keep _____ but never get any stronger.
                            (exercise)

The baby is just starting _____ his first steps.
                            (take)

I started _____ tennis at the new park.
           (play)

She stopped_____ lunch at noon.
               (eat)

She stopped_____ up so late because she needed her sleep.
               (stay)

He tried _____ the weight, but it was too heavy.
           (lift)

She tried _____ her own Kombucha as an experiment.
           (brew)

SPECIAL EXPRESSIONS

NOUN TO VERB

His **advice to study** was good.

You have a **chance to pass** the class.

He admired **her decision to take** a vacation.

Her **dream to visit** Paris was fulfilled.

I never had an **opportunity to visit** Paris.

I never got **permission to enter** the room.

My **recommendation to study** was ignored.

Their **request to leave** was granted.

Their **requirement to get** an A in the class seems unrealistic.

His **suggestion to exercise** was good.

One **way to learn** English is to watch movies.

HAVE EXPRESSIONS + VERBING

She **had a difficult time finishing** the meal.

They **had a good time scuba diving**.

She **had a hard time sleeping** last night.

She **had a problem finding** the hotel.

She **had an easy time driving** on the wide road.

They **had fun riding** the camel.

We **had no trouble following** the directions.

VERB NOUN TO VERB

She **advised her friend to take** a break.

He **convinced his parents to let** him go out.

The **job requires candidates to have** a B.A.

The teacher **allowed the students to take** a nap.

The coach **encouraged him to run** faster.

She **told her assistant to prepare** a report.

He **taught his daughter to ride** a bicycle.

The strong wind **forced the trees to bend**.

The rain **caused the river to overflow** its banks.

I **got my neighbor to help** me fix my car.

They **persuaded their friends to come**.

He **reminded his family to turn** off the lights.

LOCATION EXPRESSIONS + VERBING

She **held onto the branch praying** she wouldn't fall.

She **clung to the branch praying** she wouldn't fall.

They **ducked under the doorway descending** the narrow stairs.

The cat **crouched on the window sill watching** the birds in the yard.

He **leaned on the tree resting** in the shade.

He **lay in bed sleeping**.

She **sat on the couch dozing** off.

She **slumped on the couch dozing** off.

He **stood at the corner thinking** deep thoughts.

Special Expressions

Now you practice!
(add the preposition and verb below)

I have a chance_____ to Germany next year.
                            (fly)

My sister had a great time _____ songs in the choir.
                                  (sing)

Have we met before. I forget_____ you.
                                   (meet)

I remember _____that song. What a catchy tune!
                        (hear)

I told my best friend_____me as soon as he got home.
                                  (text)

I lay in bed _____ about my past.
                       (dream)

The rabbit crouched in the grass _____ ready to spring.
                                       (get)

I had no trouble _____ your house in the dark.
                           (find)

Her suggestion_____to bed early was good.
                         (go)

The doctor allowed his patient_____ junk food once a month.
                                     (eat)

He persuaded his wife _____ his friends at the ice skating rink.
                                (join)

She convinced me _____ her crazy diet.
                       (try)

Passive Voice

Tense	Active	Passive ("by Ben--optional)
Simple Present	Ben waters the plants.	The plants are watered. The plants get watered.
Simple Past	Ben watered the plants	The plants were watered. The plants got watered.
Simple Future	Ben will water the plants.	The plants will be watered. The plants will get watered.
Present Progressive	Ben is watering the plants.	The plants are being watered. The plants are getting watered.
Past Progressive	Ben was watereing the plants.	The plants were being watered. The plants were gettting watered.
Future Progressive	Ben will be watereing the plants.	The plants will be getting watered.
Present Perfect	Ben has watered the plants.	The plants have been watered. The plants have gotten watered.
Past Perfect	Ben had watered the plants.	The plants had been watered. The plants had gotten watered.
Future Perfect	Ben will have watered the plants.	The plants will have been watered. The plants will have gotten watered.
Present perfect progressive	Ben has been watering the plants.	The plants have been getting watered.
Past perfect progressive	Ben had been watering the plants.	The plants had been getting watered.
Future perfect progressive	Ben will have been watering the plants.	The plants will have been getting watered.
Common question forms	Is Ben watering the plants? Did Ben water the plants? Has Ben watered the plants? Will Ben water the plants?	Are the plants being watered? Were the plants watered? Have the plants been watered? Will the plants be watered?

Passive Voice

Now you practice!

Change the active to the passive below. Pay attention to tense.

Active: The movie theater shows the movie every day.
Passive: The movie is shown every day.

1. Active: The theater sells tickets for the movie.

Passive:

2. Active: The store gives a discount.

Passive:

3. Active: The restaurant makes good rice.

Passive:

4. Active: Scientists have discovered dinosaur bones there.

Passive:

5. Active: The gardener planted the tree by the river.

Passive:

When do we Use the Passive?

Rule	Example
When we don't know who does the action.	This house was built in 1980. The computer was made in China. These apples were grown in the orchards of Kandahar. Apples are grown in Bogata. This beer was imported from Germany.
When we want to hide the person who does the action. (E.g., with mistakes)	Tell me, "did you break my teapot?" Well, I saw that your teapot was broken. Caro! Did you eat the cookies? Well, the cookies were eaten.
When who does the action is not very important. (E.g., in scientific writing).	An insect was caught. Chemicals were added to the tube. Mice were exposed to the radiation. Data was observed.
With certain common verbs and expressions.	A baby is born. Men and women get married. Students are interested in class. The job is finished. The customer is satisfied. The plate is broken. The door is locked. Your parents are worried. I am dissapointed.

When do we Use the Passive?

HISTORICAL WRITING

In the passage below, underline the passive verbs.

Farming has been very important to human civilization. It was first invented in 5000 BC by people who lived in Sumeria. Seeds from wild grains were planted in the fertile ground next to the Mesopotamian rivers. The grains were harvested by people who began building houses to live in villages, which grew larger and larger as population increased. Later, iron tools were used more frequently. Shovels, harrows, and plows were manufactured by workers who became more and more skilled at metalworking.

Now you try!

Tell me about the history of an object or two. Use the passive voice as much as you can. For example, tell me where/ how it was invented or was designed or was manufactured.

Example:

This is my pencil. The pencil was invented in 1902 by Peter Pencil. This particular pencil was manufactured in China, because everything is manufactured in China. Actually, the rubber eraser was produced in Brazil. It was shipped to China to the United States in cargo ships. Finally it was given to me by the teacher.

PRACTICE WITH THE PERFECT TENSE

The present perfect tense can be used to talk both actions that happen once and actions that happened regularily.. Let's look at the following example:

Oh no! Those plants look wilted.

We use been + participle for things that happened once.

Have they been watered today?
Have _____NP_____ been _____V+Past Partiple_____ today?

Yes, they have been watered today.
Yes, _____NP_____ have been _____V+Past Partiple_____ today.

We use been + getting + past participle for repeated actions.

Have they been getting watered regularily?
Have _____NP_____ been getting _____V+Past Partiple_____ regularily?

Yes, they have been getting watered regularily.
Yes, _____NP_____ have been getting _____V+Past Partiple_____ regularily.

1. The cat looks hungry. Has she been _____ enough lately? (feed)
Has she been_____ enough today? (feed)
Answer: Yes, she_____.

2. Wow. Your car looks dirty. Has it_____enough lately (wash)
Has it_____ today?
Answer: No, it_____.

3. The dog seems anxious. Has he _____enough lately? (walk)
Has he_____today?
Answer: Yes, he _____.

4. The trash is overflowing. Has it _____ lately? (take out)
Has it _____today?
Answer: No it _____.

PREPOSITIONS OF PLACE

These prepositions help us describe the location or position of objects, people, or places in relation to each other.

Above: The book is above the shelf.

Across: The cat ran across the street.

Against: He leaned against the wall.

Among: She found her keys among the papers.

Around: They walked around the park.

Behind: The car is parked behind the house.

Below: The basement is below the ground floor.

Beside: She sat beside her friend in the class.

Between: The sandwich is between two slices of bread.

By: The painting is by the window.

In: The cat is in the box.

Inside: Please wait inside the building.

Near: The store is near the library.

Next to: The coffee mug is next to the computer.

On: The book is on the table.

Opposite: The bank is opposite the post office.

Over: The plane flew over the mountains.

Under: The shoes are under the bed.

Underneath: She found her keys underneath the couch.

Prepositions of Place

Now you practice!

Tell me where Giada's raccoon went. Make each sentence slightly longer.

Giada's raccoon went through the woods.
Giada's raccoon went through the woods and over the log.
Giada's raccoon went through the woods and over the log and under the table.

Prepositions of Place

Prepositions of Time

Fixed Times

at:
We visited her at 9:00.

clock times	at 2:00
times of day	at dusk, at dawn, at midnight
holiday periods	at Christmas

in:
We visited her in January.

months	in January
years	in 1903
morning/evening	in the morning
seasons	in the winter

on:
We visited her on Saturday.

days	on Saturday
dates	on the 19th of September (September 19th)
days+morning	on Saturday morning

Relational Times

Before:	She wanted to finish her work before the deadline.
From... to:	The store is open from 9 AM to 6 PM.
From... until/till:	The conference runs from Monday until Friday.
For:	They have been married for 10 years.
During:	It rained heavily during the night.
By:	She promised to finish the report by Friday.
After:	We'll meet at the cafe after the movie.
In:	We'll meet you at the bookstore in ten minutes.

Now you practice!
(add the preposition below)

1. The party starts_____ midnight.

2. I had a great time hanging out_____ Saturday

3. I have a meeting _____2:00 PM_____3:00 PM.

4. She goes to the gym _____ the morning.

5. The concert series will begin _____ winter.

6. We have big plans _____on the 30th of June.

7. I'll meet you at the cafe _____ 10 minutes.

8. They are planning a trip _____ summer.

9. He likes to read a book _____ bedtime.

10. My birthday is _____ October 15th.

11. It snowed _____ the night.

12. We're going to the beach _____ the weekend.

13. I can't believe my cell phone was ringing _____ the whole movie.

14. They have been married _____ over ten years.

Prepositions of Time

INSEPARABLE PHRASAL VERBS
(the prepositions cannnot be separated from the verbs)

Phrasal Verb	Definition	Example
Catch up to	reach the same level as	I need to work hard to catch up with my classmates in math.
Come across	to find or discover something by chance.	While cleaning the attic, I came across some old photographs.
Look after	to take care of or attend to someone or something.	Can you look after my cat while I'm on vacation?
Run out of	to deplete the supply of something completely.	We need to buy more milk; we've run out of it.
Settle down	to establish a stable and permanent life in one place.	After years of traveling, they decided to settle down in a quiet town.
Put up with	to tolerate or endure something unpleasant.	I don't know how she can put up with all the noise from the construction site next door.
Look forward to	to anticipate or be excited about something in the future.	I look forward to meeting you at the conference next week.
Get along	to have a good relationship with someone.	Despite their differences, they manage to get along quite well.
Live up to	to fulfill or meet someone's expectations.	She has high standards, and it's not easy to live up to them.
Put off	to delay or postpone something.	We had to put off the picnic due to the rainy weather.
Take after	to resemble or inherit certain traits from a family member.	She really takes after her mother, both in looks and personality.
Turn up	to arrive or appear, often unexpectedly.	He didn't RSVP, but he still turned up at the party.
Run into	to encounter or meet someone unexpectedly.	I ran into an old friend at the supermarket yesterday.
Go on	continue (as a show)	The show must go on!

Inseparable Phrasal Verbs

Now you practice

Fill in the blanks with the phrasal verbs from the preceeding page

1. After years of traveling, they decided to _____ in a quiet town.

2. I need to work hard to _____ with my classmates in math.

3. We had to _____ the picnic due to the rainy weather.

4. Can you _____ my cat while I'm on vacation?

5. Despite their differences, they manage to _____ quite well.

6. She really _____ her mother, both in looks and personality.

7. We've _____ of milk; we need to buy more.

8. I didn't RSVP, but I still _____ at the party.

9. I _____ to meeting you at the conference next week.

10. He didn't _____ for the job interview on time.

11. She has high standards, and it's not easy to _____ them.

12. The show must _____ despite the technical difficulties.

13. While cleaning the attic, I _____ some old photographs.

14. He couldn't _____ with all the noise from the construction site next door.

15. I _____ an old friend at the supermarket yesterday.

SEPARABLE PHRASAL VERBS

the verb can be separated from the preposition

Phrasal	Separable form	Inseparable form
find out (discover)	I found an important fact out.	I found out an important fact.
set up (arrange)	She set the room up.	She set up the room.
bring up (introduce a topic for discussion)	I brought an interesting topic up in my conversation with her.	I brought up an interesting topic in my conversation with her.
take on (challenge)	She took the challenge on of climbing the snowy mountain.	She took on the challenge of climbing the snowy mountain.
turn down (lower volume reject)	It's too loud in here, can you turn the volume down?	I asked her to the movies, but she turned down my offer.
turn up (show up/ flip)* Different meanings	I was very busy, so it was late before I turned up at the party.	The pancake is starting to burn. You should turn the edges up in the pan.
tell off (speak sharply to)	It was a great joy to tell my boss off before I quit.	It was a great joy to tell off my boss before I quit.
let down (dissapoint)	I study as hard as I can because I don't want to let my parents down.	I study as hard as I can because I don't want to let down my parents.
take up (adopt a hobby)	I have a lot of free time, so I'm thinking that I want to take knitting up.	I have a lot of free time, so I'm thinking I want to take up knitting.

Separable Phrasal Verbs

Now you practice

Pick <u>five</u> of the prhasal verbs on the previous page. Write two sentences for each one. In one sentence, use the separable verb. In the other sentence, use the non-seperable verb.

Example: take on

He <u>took on</u> the responsibility of fatherhood.
He <u>took</u> the responsibility of fatherhood <u>on</u>.

1. Phrasal:

* _____

* _____

2 Phrasal:

* _____

* _____

3 Phrasal:

* _____

* _____

4. Phrasal:

* _____

* _____

5. Phrasal:

* _____

* _____

PHRASALS WITH COMMON VERBS

BE

be with	be into	be on it
to accompany, to be romantically involved with	be interested in	be taking care of a problem
I didn't know he was with her.	I'm into film.	The faucet is leaking, but I'm on it.
be on top of	be out	be over
to be taking care of a problem	be outside/ be openly gay	be tired of something
I'm on top of my homework.	John's out, but his partner isn't.	I'm so over this book.

HAVE

have it out	have on	have it in for
argue	wear	want revenge against
They've been having it out all night.	That's a nice outfit you have on.	He really has it in for his old boss.
have at it	have over (seperable)	
try to solve a problem	invite	
Want to help me fix my car! There, have at it.	We had the neighbors over for lunch.	

GO

go over	give a going over	go out with
review	yell at	date
Let's go over the homework.	She really gave him a going over!	She's been going out with Jose for 3 months!
go on and on	go at it	go into
speak incessently	fight	explain in detail
She kept going on and on about her new car.	Boy! They've been going at it all night!	Let's go into the perfect tenses.

MAKE

make up	make up* (n)	make over* (often n)
reconcile/ reschedule	cosmetics	redesign
I'm so glad we managed to make up.	She's really good at doing her make up.	This house needs a total make over.
If you miss the exam, you can make it up.		
make with	make it	make out with
hurry up	succeed	kiss passionately
Make with your speech already!	He made it as a banker.	He made out with his girlfriend.

234

COME

come around	come down (n)	come into
visit	to be depressed after feeling happy	inherit
He comes around about once every two weeks.	After the holidays, returning to work is a bit of a come down.	She came into a fortune after her grandfather passed away.
come back	come with	come about
return	accompany	happen
It was nice seeing you. I hope you come back and visit us again soon.	Will you come with me to the dance on Friday?	How did that come about?

PUT

put on	put out	put off
wear	place outside	annoy
I'd better put my shirt on before I go outside.	Can you put the trash out please.	His personality really puts me off.
put down	put back	put up with
insult/ set on the floor	return to its place	tolerate
Her husband is so mean. He always puts her down in front of the children. You can put your glass down on the table.	Can you put this book back please.	This song is terrible. I find it so hard to put up with it.

BREAK

break down	break up with	break into
(malfunction)	(discontinue a romantic relationship)	(enter without permission)
My computer broke down and now I need a new one.	They dated for a year before they broke up.	The thief broke into the house.
break open	break out	break off
(open a package)	(escape)	(similar to break up with: to discontinue)
He broke the box open to get his computer out.	The prisoners broke out of the prison.	Let's break off the story here and read more next week.

PREPOSITION DICE GAME
Roll two dice.

(Or use your phone). Practice making sentences using slang phrasals. Use the vocabulary on the following page.

DICE 1		DICE 2	
1	be or have	1	with
2	make	2	out
3	come	3	over
4	put	4	in
5	go	5	on
6	break	6	down

Sentences

1

2

3

4

5

6

Quick Practice

Fill in the blanks with the appropriate phrasal verb.

1. She's really _____ painting. It's her favorite hobby.
   a) with
   b) into
   c) on it
   d) on top of

2. The news _____ the radio just now. Did you catch it?
   a) is over
   b) comes about
   c) comes with
   d) is on

3. We can't _____ the meeting later. It's important to discuss these issues today.
   a) make up
   b) come into
   c) come back
   d) break off

4.. I always _____ my keys on the hook immedientlhy when I get home.
   a) put out
   b) break down
   c) put back
   d) break up with

5. She _____ the dress and looked stunning at the party.
   a) put on
   b) put up with
   c) go on and on
   d) have it in for

6. We need to _____ this issue before it becomes a major problem.
   a) break into
   b) go over
   c) come about
   d) come with

7. The students _____ a challenging assignment during the exam.
   a) went on and on
   b) came into
   c) had it out
   d) broke down

Most Common Irregular Verbs

be, was, been
bear, bore, born
beat, beat, beaten
begin, began, begun
bite, bit, bitten
blow, blew, blown
break, broke, broken
bring, brought, brought
build, built, built
buy, bought, bought
catch, caught, caught
cast, cast, cast
choose, chose, chosen
come, came, come
cost, cost, cost
cut, cut, cut
deal, dealt, dealt
dig, dug, dug
do, did, done
draw, drew, drawn
drive, drove, driven
drink, drank, drunk
eat, ate, eaten
fall, fell, fallen
feel, felt, felt
find, found, found
fly, flew, flown
freeze, froze, frozen
get, got, gotten
give, gave, given
go, went, gone
grow, grew, grown
hang, hung, hung
have, had, had
hear, heard, heard
hide, hid, hidden
hit, hit, hit
hold, held, held
hurt, hurt, hurt
keep, kept, kept
know, knew, known

lay, laid, laid
lead, led, led
leave, left, left
let, let, let
lie, lay, lain
light, lit, lit
make, made, made
mean, meant, meant
meet, met, met
pay, paid, paid
prove, proved, proven
put, put, put
read, read, read
ride, rode, ridden
ring, rang, rung
rise, rose, risen
run, ran, run
say, said, said
see, saw, seen
sell, sold, sold
send, sent, sent
set, set, set
show, showed, shown
shut, shut, shut
sing, sang, sung
sink, sank, sunk
sit, sat, sat
slide, slid, slid
speak, spoke, spoken
spread, spread, spread
stand, stood, stood
steal, stole, stolen
stick, stuck, stuck
swear, swore, sworn
swim, swam, swum
teach, taught, taught
tear, tore, torn
tell, told, told
think, thought, thought
throw, threw, thrown
wake, woke, woken
wear, wore, worn
wet, wet, wet
win, won, won

Most Common Irregular Verbs

Add up
Back up
Blow up
Break in
Bring up
Brush up on
Build up
Call back
Call in
Call off
Calm down
Carry on
Carry out
Catch up
Check out
Check in
Clear up
Come across
Come down with
Come up
Come up with
Cut back on
Cut off
Cut down on
Do over
Do without
Drop by
Drop off
Eat out
Fill in
Fill out
Find out
Get by
Get over
Give away
Give back
Give in
Give up
Go on
Go over
Go up
Hand in
Hang out

Hold on
Hold up
Keep up
Let down
Look after
Look forward to
Look up
Look up to
Make up
Pass away
Pick out
Pick up
Put away
Put off
Put out
Run away
Run into
Run out of
Set up
Settle down
Show up
Sit down
Stand up
Take after
Take in
Take off
Take out
Think over
Throw away
Try on
Turn around
Turn down
Turn off
Turn on
Turn up
Walk in on
Wake up
Wake up to
Wait for
Wash up
Watch out
Work out

Made in United States
Orlando, FL
27 February 2024